# *Live from Atlantic City*

# Live from Atlantic City:
# The History of the Miss America Pageant Before, After and in Spite of Television

## A. R. Riverol

Bowling Green State University Popular Press
Bowling Green, Ohio 43403

Library of Congress Catalogue Card No.: 92-81612

ISBN: 0-87972-557-5 Clothbound
       0-87972-558-3 Paperback

Cover design by Gary Dumm

# Contents

# Acknowledgments

This book could not have been possible without the help, encouragement, guidance, support, and resources of many mentors, teachers, friends, colleagues, informants, and family members. Their names appear below in grateful acknowledgment.

Special thanks must first be given to Terry Moran, without whose tutelage, firm support, and encouragement this study would never have been completed. Professor Moran taught this investigator that scholarship means discipline, that goals need focus, that knowledge needs structure, and so much more.

Henry Perkinson's guidance is, likewise, more than just appreciated. Before and during the writing of this book, Professor Perkinson was and continued to be a respected guide in my quest for knowledge. Henry's scholarship and gentle manner have been an inspiration.

Also to be acknowledged at New York University: Neil Postman and Chris Nystrom who inspired me to question; to Robert Berlin for his critical eye and much-missed ironic wit; to Phillip Hosay for teaching me that histories should be more akin to paintings than to encyclopedias; to Jean Maculaitis for a life-time of love and guidance; to Janice Gorn for structure. Last, and of importance, to the memory of Professor Sidney Gross, who started me on this journey but could not be here to see its end.

The help and support of the following friends and colleagues are greatly and deeply appreciated: first and foremost, Vasu Varadhan and Janet Lewis who prodded me on when I was ready to call it quits. Thanks also to Bob Albrecht, John Bell, John Cooke, Moishe Botwinik, Elspeth Corrigan, Myrna Frommer, Margot Hardenbergh, Paul Lippert, Millie Livingstone, Susan Mausehart, Tom Mullen, Dan Robinson, Jay Rosen, Mona Scheraga, Lance Strate, and Carol Wendt.

Special thanks are extended to the following informants for their time and invaluable help: Karen Aarons, Evelyn Ay, Marian Bergeron, Jean Bray, Laura Bridges, Joe Cook, Lenora Slaughter Frapart, John Koushouris, Patricia LaTerra, Lee Meriwether, Adrian Phillips, Laurie Schaeffer, Jean Seber, Vonda Van Dyke, Jacqueline Walker, Sharlene Wells, John Zerbe. Also, Marie Boyd at the Atlantic City Library and Emily Angelitis at A.C. Nielsen.

Special, special, special thanks to Therese Hanley, Miss NJ 1980: second in Atlantic City but first in this book. Without Trés, I never would have been introduced to the world of pageants.

Last, but by no means least, a special thanks must go to Frank Sciallo for his support, patience, and encouragement; to my sister Rita, Paul, Paul Jr. and Christine; and especially to my mother, Alfreda Riverol, and my father, Armando Riverol, to whom I owe everything.

# Foreword

It is September. It is just about the stroke of midnight. Unseen throngs of half-bored people turn on their televisions or switch channels before calling it a night. Millions of others, however, have been glued to their sets for some time. What is this communal rite that finds a common audience from such uncommon backgrounds? That event is the *Miss America Pageant*. Yes, Miss America. Whether to laugh with or at, scores of curious voyeurs or obsessed groupies all over the United States religiously watch the *Miss America Pageant* each September. Just as sure as the swallows return habitually to Capistrano, the traditional cycle of Miss America viewing recurs as a precursor to school, football, and other such American rituals of autumn. In the interim, from one September until the next, thousands of girls between the ages of eighteen and twenty-six begin that yearly journey to Atlantic City. From the thousands competing in local and state pageants only fifty find their way to the stage at Convention Hall. September once more, the cycle begins again.

Whether we admit it or not, once a year (and only once), the country comes down with pageant fever. This fever, however, is most times more torrid than the pageant folks would prefer. On or about the first week in September a plethora of articles bombard the newsstands. Splashing the covers of popular magazines, periodicals, and supermarket tabloids their headlines declare: "Won By a Nose," "The Miss America Uproar: What it Says About us All," "Vanessa the Undressa Loses Crown," "Here She Comes, Broke," "Miss America Stole My Husband," and "There She Grows...Miss America Packs on Hefty 20 Lbs.," among many, many others.[1] Articles such as these, while entertaining at best and laughable at least, deal mostly with pageant scandal. In essence, they are "balloon poppers," which try to deflate some great American myth. It is perhaps this sensational approach to the *Miss America Pageant* that has diminished a greater consideration for either scholarly research or serious discussion on the topic.

A review of the literature revealed that scholarly writings on the *Miss America Pageant* are scant. Among the noteworthy studies conducted is one by social historian, Lois Banner.[2] Banner's study dedicates a portion of a chapter of her book, *American Beauty*, to the *Miss America Pageant*.

Other authors have focused not on the sociological implications of the *Miss America Pageant*, but rather on its role as a lucrative by-product of Atlantic City's rise as a resort. Such books include *By the Beautiful Sea:*

the *Rise and High Times of that Great Resort, Atlantic City, So Young...So Gay*, and *Atlantic City: 125 Years of Ocean Madness*.[3]

Still others have chosen to write on the experiences of Miss America, the woman. Frank Deford, for example, chronicles the pageant and its "queens."[4] *Miss America Through the Looking Glass*, by Nancie Martin, chronicles the *Miss America Pageant* in a similar (though digested) manner as Deford. The book addresses some Miss Americas not yet crowned as of the printing of Deford's book. Martin, writing at times with tongue-in-cheek flair, basically restates much of the extant material on Miss America, probing no new aspects of inquiry, and failing to "make good" on the promise made by her tantalizing subtitle: *The Story Behind the Scenes*.[5]

Other books focusing on Miss America include *Sharing the Crown* by Marjorie Ford.[6] In this book, Judith Ford's (Miss America 1979) mother tells of the experiences that Miss America and her family go through before, during, and after her coronation. Perhaps the most sensational book on Miss America is *Hype and Glory*, in which the author William Goldman, a former judge, breaches his trust and confidentiality as judge by telling a nasty tale of back stage gossip.[7] Other books written by Miss Americas themselves dealing with their experiences include those by Jacques Mercer (1949), Cheryl Prewitt (1981), and Bess Myerson (1945).[8]

While these books are essays full of colorful anecdotes, few scholarly studies have dealt with Miss America empirically. One study conducted by Henry Pang, appearing in the *Journal of Popular Culture*, analyzes the physical attributes of the Miss America winners from 1921-1968 as well as their geographic origins. According to Pang, "Trends and developments can be used in analyzing and understanding societal and cultural aspects in different societies."[9] Using such similar data about previous winners each year in recent years, George Miller, a statistician from Northern Illinois University, "handicaps" the winner of that year's pageant—a prediction that some pageant hopefuls feel works against them.[10]

Documentaries have also been made on different aspects of the beauty pageant. ABC's *20/20* reported on juvenile pageants.[11] A documentary film with the title *Miss...or Myth?* played at the New York Film Forum on September 16-22, 1987.[12] The film, publicized as an "exposé of the Miss California Pageant," endeavored to make a connection between the exploitation of women through pageants and rape.[13]

In view of all of the above interest and speculation concerning pageants in general and the Miss America Pageant in particular, it is logical to state that any event that can boast of being an American tradition while at the same time be considered a worthy enough opponent by its adversaries; any event that can cause such hoopla in both popular and intellectual circles demands closer, further, and more in-depth scrutiny. Obviously (or not so obviously) there is something about this seemingly innocuous pageant that raises an eye brow, a giggle, or a picket sign. As such, its social significance cannot be dismissed as trivial. As media theorist Neil Postman writes, "an analysis of the meaning of 'beauty contests' could all by itself, occupy weeks of constructive academic work under the rubric of 'mass culture studies.'"[14]

The goal of this book is to take that closer, further, and in-depth look. To this end, the book chronicles the metamorphosis of the *Miss America Pageant* from a live, local contest in 1921 to an annually televised national event watched by millions.[15] Specifically, the idea (and by consequence the point of view) for this book was sparked by the often overlooked premise that before the Pageant ever came to us "live *from* Atlantic City," it first existed live *in* Atlantic City.

To most people, the Pageant is nothing more than a non-committal entertainment event experienced in what can be called the secondary media environment of television. Pageant devotees argue that it is because of this second hand, once removed, incomplete experience that (mis)conceptions about the Pageant are made. Those whose vocation or avocation revolve around the *Miss America Pageant* (and there are many) would propose that to experience the Pageant you have to live the Pageant, and that means being in Atlantic City, all week, live and in person.

To them, to experience Miss America one needs to breathe in not only the salty Atlantic Ocean air, but also the fumes of hair spray in Convention Hall. To experience Miss America one needs to feel the familial ambience of pageant gossip so prevalent in pre-pageant parties. To see the pageant at home on television is the chance to miss the handicapping of pageant hopefuls over cocktail or blackjack tables. Television audiences will miss the gaggles of pageant mavins sequined like last year's Christmas tree scurrying to Convention Hall while shielding their bullet-proof hairdos from the night breeze with a pageant program. The homeviewer also misses how occasionally these garish groups will of necessity stop to disinter a spiked heel from the planks of the Boardwalk. As if to add further hazard to this odyssey, the obstacle course to Convention Hall must be hobbled, one shoe in hand, while scrupulously dodging the homeless, the hucksters, the hawkers, the hustlers, and the hookers flanking the Boardwalk.

To be in Atlantic City for pageant week is to see Miss America "wannabees" in all sizes, shapes, colors, ages, and sexual persuasions parading on the fringes of mainstream pageant society in their assorted tiaras, banners, and store-bought pageant titles. To be home is to miss the back stage hysteria after the top ten are announced. Those in Atlantic City at the right place and time have been privy to the emergence of claws from where manicured fingernails once existed. They have witnessed the binging of emaciated losers on high caloric foods, and sometimes even on sour grapes. To be home is to miss the sight of last year's winner tossed aside like a rag by photographers more interested in this year's winner. To be home is to miss the bark of the program vendors, the bitchy commentary of drunken spectators, and the gate-crashing lies of back stage groupies.

For better or worse, to Pageant aficionados, the two hours flashed to the remote corners of America one Saturday night in September via television is but a minute sliver of the total Miss American pie. This seemingly insignificant detail takes on monumental proportions when one considers that it is a fact many people connected with television don't comprehend. To a majority of Pageant fans, the thought of Miss America existing without Atlantic City or vice versa is simply unthinkable. Their perspective on the Pageant is drawn from the illogical realms of tradition, invested emotion, and idealism. Logical suggestions dealing with the improvement of ratings, the need for a dramatic build-up, or a change of time slot or location are usually politely tolerated, considered, and then just as politely shrugged off. This, of course, has been known to cause great befuddlement in the minds of many an "expert."

In light of the above, this book examines the live *Miss America Pageant* in its primary media environment, that is, live and in real time and space *in* Atlantic City, New Jersey. Television or other media coverage is mentioned only in how it affected the structure of the live event. Furthermore, because of the volume of data, the book is delimited to examining a structured sample of all pageants beginning with the first pageant in 1921 and then every ten years through 1953 (the year before the advent of television coverage). From there, every ten years commencing with the advent of television in 1954 through the present (1991) will likewise be described.

It is the author's hope that this panoramic picture of the pageant's past is painted vividly enough yet objectively enough to allow scholars delving into questions important to the study of popular culture, fans of the Pageant, and those who have formed a love/hate relationship with this (un)popular Miss to be both entertained and informed.

With all of these odds and endless ends in mind:

FORWARD!

A.R. Riverol

# Chapter I
# Preliminary Thoughts

Although to some it might seem that the concept of the beauty pageant is as old as sexism itself; and although the images of teary-eyed ingenues walking down a runway along with other such pageant associated kitsch have become so cliché as to make us assume that they were created some time during Genesis, the fact is, that the genre in its present incarnation and form is a relatively new invention. If the prehistorics judged their women in loin cloth, beauty of fang and figure, and primordial screams before dragging them into the cave, there is no anecdotal or iconic evidence.[1]

Indeed, as will be demonstrated in this chapter, pageants as we know them today could not have existed anytime in our history outside the last hundred or so years. Before then, social conditions made the respectable, institutional, flagrant, and profitable exposition of scantily clad girls before a paying audience inconceivable. That one girl from the many would be picked from the rest like a prize cow, a slave, or a coveted piece of candy made it not only difficult for the genre to emerge, but outright impossible. In times when duels were fought over a maiden's virtue; in times when men guarded their women like treasures; in times when puritanical and religious fervor permeated society, it was unfathomable that daughters and sisters would parade before others for indepth inspection and approval. Whores and slaves could undergo such demeaning scrutiny, but not proper ladies. As such, the question of whether or not to have a pageant or whether they were right or wrong, was never a question at all. It would take many centuries and the proper social conditions for pageants as we know them to not only become a respectable and socially acceptable form, but also to become at all.

While it cannot be argued that historically there have been women (and yes, also men) who have used their looks as a means to an end, the practice (an art form in itself), has operated one on one, informally, and most often discretely, unlike pageants. Nonetheless, some critics argue that these labels, *modus operandi*, and ethos are also inherent in formal pageants, and hence, for better or worse are merely reflections of the existing social order. As such, a look at some famous stories of myth and legend dealing with this theme, which will be called Beauty Triumphant, provides valuable insight into two opposing perspectives on pageants: pageants as a legitimate part of the historical social order, and adversely, pageants as exploiters of women.

*The Myths of Beauty Triumphant*

### Cinderella

Literature and history swell with the uncountable stories of the Beauty overcoming the Beast, the Beauty winning the heart of the high and mighty, the Beauty saving the day or the kingdom, and countless other tales with Beauty as a central and pivotal force. One example is the story of Cinderella. In this story, Cinderella, because of her beauty, is chosen from among the ugly step sisters and also-rans to live happily ever after with the catch of all catches, the Prince himself. The story implies among other things that it is quite conceivable for a girl of humble origins to climb the social ladder with no tools but her beauty and small feet. Based on what the story infers, these traits are much coveted and sought after female attributes. In her study, *American Beauty*, social historian Lois Banner touches upon this point and how it is embodied in beauty contests:

> The history of beauty contests tells us much about American attitudes toward physical appearances and women's expected roles. Rituals following set procedures, beauty contests have long existed to legitimize the Cinderella mythology for women, to make it seem that beauty is all a woman needs for success and, as a corollary, that beauty ought to be a major pursuit of all women.[2]

### Esther

Another example of Beauty Triumphant can be found in the Bible. In this classic story, Esther, the heroine, depends upon her beauty to get access to the king. Though beautiful, she must, nonetheless, compete with other lovelies for the king's undivided affection. So that she might stand out and be chosen over the other contenders, Esther is primed and primped by the eunuch, Hegai. Some might propose that this story bears proof that a form of beauty pageant existed in ancient times, and further, that Hegai has the honor of being the first of a long line of pageant trainers.

Others might suggest this story merely demonstrates the model upon which the beauty contest is based. In this perspective, women are seen as helpless chattel: objects molded by men to be chosen by men, and thereafter to please men. Furthermore, many pageant critics point out that the grooming of contestants for pageants seems ironic at best and hypocritical at worst. It is an indictment of a system that aspires to lofty ideals such as scholarship and ingenuity, and yet condones the cultivation of artifice. How odd it seems that in many cases, it takes months of training, prepping, and guidance as well as countless dollars in gowns, costumes, and even surgery to achieve that natural All-American, girl next door look.

In her book *Femininity*, Susan Brownmiller echoes this pageant antagonist's point of view. She writes:

> Women in our society are forced daily to compete for male approval, enslaved by ludicrous beauty standards that we ourselves are conditioned to take seriously and to accept.[3]

Substitute the word men or male with power brokers of any kind, and the same holds true with pageants. Of course, Esther went on to save her people through her intelligence. Persistent critics insist, however, that her entree to the world of power would have been precluded if not for her looks.

### Scheherazade

The story of Scheherazade provides another example of a beautiful woman's use of her beauty to gain influence and success. In general, the tale tells of a Middle Eastern king with a large, lusty, and insatiable appetite for things of the sexual order. Each night the king would bed one of the many lovely women of his harem. After he had had his way and was sated, the girl was discarded and condemned to death. Obviously, one lost more than the crown in this contest. One lost the head upon which the crown itself would sit. Enter Scheherazade. Although she was beautiful, Scheherazade was also intelligent, wily, and talented. As she lay in the king's arms after the loving, she softly and sensually whispered into his ear a wondrous and magical tale thereby keeping him awake, interested, and yearning for more—stories. Whether it was her sexual charms or her story telling abilities that kept her alive for one more night will never be known. Whatever the case, myth insists that it was her tales and not her tail that kept her close to the king's ear and heart for one thousand and one nights. It is assumed, that on the one thousand and second night, Scheherazade became the queen, living happily ever after.

Pageant supporters might flaunt this story as a pageant prototype, insisting that the girl succeeded based on her talent presentation, intelligence, and ability to speak extemporaneously, and not on her looks alone. To them, this example provides proof that Scheherazade, just as pageant women, was the one fully in control. These women have a goal and use their abilities and looks to reach it.

Others might argue that this story merely illustrates that the price of the crown for this and other women has been at the expense of their integrity and identity. These women are powerless to succeed without the use of sexuality or craft. To succeed, they must mouth words that, although are not necessarily in their hearts, are, nonetheless, pleasing to the ears of those with the power to change or shape their lives. Whether it be life, as in Scheherazade's case, or simply a dream realized, there are those who would exploit the dreams, bodies, and talents of starry-eyed youths by dangling before them the carrot of hope. It is a lesson, some say, that is ingrained deeply both in the minds of the exploiter and the exploited. It is a time-tested method that is tried, true, and effective. Because of its commonplace practice, it is taken as a given fact of life. What recourse was offered to Scheherazade? Play or die. Critics of pageant systems say that contestants today are given the same unspoken choice. Supporters, on the other hand, insist that it is not the choice to "not fail" that pageants offer, but rather the opportunity to succeed.

# 4    Live from Atlantic City

*The Judgement of Paris*

Perhaps the classical tale that most closely resembles a beauty pageant in form is the mythological story, "The Judgement of Paris." As such, it offers ample opportunity for drawing parallels. The story opens on Mount Olympus during a party in which every god and goddess was present except Chaos who was not invited for obvious reasons. Insulted and disgruntled, Chaos decided to throw a little bash of her own to compete for the attention of god and man. This she did by throwing into the middle of the party the infamous golden apple of discord which was inscribed "To the Most Beautiful." What resulted was indeed chaos. Where once beauty might have been uncontested (you either were or weren't) now a hierarchy of beauty was forced to exist. That there was a most beautiful implied that there was a second most beautiful and so on down the line until rock bottom was hit with "Ugliest." In "The Judgement of Paris," none of the goddesses wanted the distinction of being anything less than the most beautiful. Goddesses, being vain and petty creatures (unlike their male counterparts) went to all extremes to be chosen the prototype of perfection.

After a preliminary elimination, three goddesses were chosen for the finals. They were Athena, Hera, and Aphrodite. The gods, not being foolish, selected a mortal man to decide the final outcome. His name was Paris, the first of a long list of men judging the worth of women. The three goddesses offered Paris bribes. Aphrodite offered Paris Helen of Troy, the most beautiful (though married) mortal woman. Paris chose Aphrodite as the winner, and the rest, as they say, is history—the Trojan War. The implication in this story that beauty (Aphrodite) wins over intellect (Athena) and authority (Hera) and that the pursuit of beauty (Helen) as well as the use of beauty for profit or position was worth the price of dishonesty and war, suggests that the misplacement of society's priorities can cause social ruin. Needless, to say, humankind must have seen the folly wrought by Chaos, for beauty pageants of this sort were never again to be produced until modern times.

*Pageant Precursors*

It has been said that although technologies (inventions, discoveries, and so forth) open the door to social change, a society must walk through that door to reap the benefits. Take the classic case of one technology, the wheel. No one can argue as to the effect the wheel has had on human civilization. Ironically, the Aztec culture, though familiar with the wheel, did not choose to walk through that metaphorical door. Hence, the wheel was only used in that culture as a toy. Old World cultures, on the other hand, exploited the technology in different ways, harnessing its power to both roll the species forward as well as to crush, grind, and devastate peoples and places. Some would argue that in Old World cultures, the conditions were right for people of vision to tap the potential of the technology. In pre-Colombian America neither the need, nor, by consequence, the visionaries were there (at least in the case of the wheel).

It is important to note that, as alluded to above, social conditions and need alone are not the only factors to instigate change or discovery. It takes people in tune to the ebbs and flows of social conditions to grasp the moment and take that fateful step through that "evolving door."

Just as with the wheel, in hindsight, one could list endless other inventions, discoveries, business ventures, fads, cures, art forms, techniques, better mouse traps, and what-nots that might have been—if circumstances had been right; that could have been—if the need had arisen; that should have been—if the tree had been discerned poking its leafy head from the midst of the camouflaging proverbial forest. Though not as earth-moving or in the same scope as the invention of the wheel, the same can be said about the beauty pageant genre. As far as the bathing beauty contest was concerned, those circumstances did not exist until the last hundred or so years. As will be discussed below, the seed of the idea was present, however, in other similar types of events. The beauty pageant was a concept merely awaiting the proper time or person to awaken it from its germinating sleep.

Although Banner does not negate the nineteenth century origin of the beauty pageant, she does argue against the beauty *contest's* uniqueness to our culture. She cites several examples to substantiate her claim. Among the non-American beauty contests she cites is one taking place in the Vienna Annenfest. In this contest, the participant who collected the most tickets from men present at the festival would be chosen the winner. Another foreign entry into the annals of beauty contests is the *Fetes des Blanchisseuses* in which Parisian laundresses elected the most beautiful among them.[4]

Banner offers other examples of beauty contests existing in different incarnations prior to 1920, the year of the first *Miss America Pageant*. Among the examples are May Day celebrations in which, according to Banner, "...[nineteenth century English and American girls] crowned their favorite friend Queen of the May."[5] Banner also offers as example Twelfth Night parties held twelve days after Christmas to commemorate the visitation of the Magi. At these parties a ring and a bean were baked into separate cakes. The man who found the ring and the woman who found the bean were chosen king and queen of the evening.[6]

Still another example of a contest discussed by Banner in which a king and or a queen was chosen can be found in the nineteenth-century tournaments, events made popular by the publishing of the novel *Ivanhoe* in 1829. For the most part, tournaments were held in the southern states. In these tournaments, male competitors, while riding on horseback, attempted to spear rings from a hook as well as to mangle a figure painted on a board by shooting at it or slashing it with a saber. The man with the most lanced rings and/or who inflicted the most harm on the target would have the honor of naming the queen of the tournament. Losers chose the attendants.[7]

*Selections and Elections*

It cannot be argued that contests such as the ones mentioned have existed perhaps since the beginning of civilization when some lucky gal or guy was elected because of his or her beauty, at random, or by chance to be thrown into a volcano. Though these contests had the choosing of a winner (usually a woman) in common with contemporary beauty pageants, the similarity stops there. Though to some extent they are pageant precursors, they are not that genre unique in origin to both America and modern times.

Selections, elections, and other contests designed to choose one from the many are based on the inequity of popularity, the whim of fate, or at times from the performance of tasks unrelated to the specific contested title. Pageants, on the other hand, base the selection of winners on the decision of judges who must operate under formal rules and criteria as well as on the basis of informal traditions and standards. That the practice of selecting and electing kings, queens, and other winners still exists today does not disqualify them as valid forms or competitions, however. Instead they exist as forms unto themselves which when contrasted with pageants share commonalities but are, nonetheless, quite different. Just as in some point in history prehistoric man co-existed with homo sapien, so too do these beauty pageant precursors and prototypes co-exist with the beauty pageant.

At worst, these type of contests conjure up "B" movie clichés of casting couches and back stage intrigue. In effect, these types of contests are populated by grifters, scam artists, and other opportunists motivated by lucre and greed at the expense of starry-eyed innocents. For many, their encounters with these types of contests evoke bitter memories remembered with neither nostalgia nor Rockwellian charm. Instead the memories come back as hard lessons in life learned after a night or nights of tears and broken dreams. How many of us can remember some contest in which the winner was chosen not by merit but by how many loud-clapping, wolf-whistling friends he or she packed into the auditorium? How many of us can cite a contest in which the winner captures the crown not on merit but on how many tickets or raffle chances he or she sold? How many of us have observed the heartbreaking sight of some less-than-pretty, less-than-talented would-be model taking a pointless waddle down a runway? What were the qualifying factors? There were none other than payment of some hefty entry fee. These contests, obviously, are not charitable or equitable but rather, profitable. The bait, more often than not, is the groundless promise of a career in show biz, exposure to talent agents, a contract, and on and on and on.

Not all selections and elections are seedy or exploitative, however. Some of these types of contests at their best are intermeshed into the tapestry of American tradition. One need only think of senior year in most high schools across the country when some sort of queen and king are selected among the other pimply faces who have yet to attain that post-pubescent beauty and popularity of the winners. Think of the Senior Polls in which a boy and a girl (usually the same two) are selected Most Attractive.

For other such examples, one need only think of churches, lodges, hospitals, schools, and other organizations who yearly select, elect, or acknowledge one among the many. In these instances, the selection, election, or acknowledgement is arrived at by a task or tasks accomplished in benefit of the organization, *e.g.*, who sold the most raffle tickets, who put in the most hours, who contributed the most, and so forth. These types of selections or elections are usually for charitable causes. While being chosen Mrs. PTA or Cub Scout of the Year offers its tinge of pride, the goal and the real enjoyment is not in attaining the crown or the prize but in the actual process of raising of the funds.

Whatever the title, whether it be the selection of a belle by newspapers as was practiced in nineteenth century America, the election by applause-o-meter of Queen for a Day, or selection of a parade's Grand Marshal, though sharing similarities, selections and elections are as akin to modern beauty pageants as oranges are to grapefruits.[8] While selections and elections have existed throughout history and continue through the present, beauty pageants depended on other social and historical factors for their birth.

What was it about modern times that made the beauty pageant genre a possibility? Inversely, what was it about previous times that made its genesis impossible? Some of those factors will be discussed in the following section.

### The Fairest of the Fair

The Industrial Revolution of the nineteenth century brought with it an age of leisure for the working and middle classes. Time spent with one's nose at the grindstone was cut by industrialization. Man, woman, and child were liberated by the machine which gave them added time to reap what was once available only to the privileged few: the right to do nothing at all. As such, industries associated with leisure sprang up, including carnivals, fairs, circuses, musical theatre, Wild West Shows, amusement parks, and sea side resorts.

Women were among the many gimmicks used to attract a paying audience to the new world of relaxation, amusement, and entertainment. Consequently, they became the cogs and wheels that propelled the leisure industries. It is ironic that leisure would create a venue of employment for women. By the score they came out of the kitchens into the marketplace. They hung up their clothes lines and joined the chorus lines as well as the assembly lines. They were emancipated from the status of domestic work horses and soon, as models, became clothes horses.

Just as freaks, animals, and Indians were flaunted by Barnum, Cody and others, so too were women. For the amusement of an audience, dogs, flowers, babies, and birds were judged in their respective field at contests held by P.T. Barnum. In 1854, taking the contest gimmick one step further, Barnum initiated what many consider to be the first actual beauty pageant. In the 1854 contest, women paraded before judges who appraised their faces and figures. In another ten years, the human auction blocks would be closed. However, the birth of the beauty pageant, some might argue, had replaced them using sex rather than race as a selling point. In Barnum's contest, the winner, if married, would win a diamond tiara. If single, she would win a dowry.[9] The contest turned out to be a failure because the only ones to apply were women of "questionable reputations." The exploitation of America's young women had to be done within the parameters of respectability. America's best representative product had to be labeled "Maid in the USA." Taking the cue from his failure, Barnum changed his format, asking that instead of appearing in person, a contestant would instead be judged from her daguerreotype submission. The idea was quite successful and popular. According to Banner, by the end of the century, the photographic beauty contest was used by a large number of newspapers as a publicity gimmick.[10] The time for beauty as a legitimate, socially approved, financial commodity had arrived, transforming women from the prize to the priced. By the end of the century, the beauty contest had attained a degree of respectability. Where once only wicked queens could ask who was the fairest of them all, the newly found respectability of the beauty contest made it acceptable for the girl next door to contemplate such matters.

### The Birth of Venus

Although beauty contests featuring respectable young women had become mainstream, it would take other social changes, attitudes, and innovations for the *bathing* beauty form to emerge. Were it not for those changes, the beauty contest genre might have remained in the order of either the selection/election or photographic type.

Perhaps one of the most significant social changes to occur in the nineteenth century with regard to the generation of the beauty pageant form was the changes in attitude about bathing. Although swimming and bathing were part of civilization's historic heritage as a means of cleansing and regeneration, their use began declining in Europe in the late fourteen hundreds. Not willing to embrace or be associated with the Moorish tradition of bathing, "a Queen of Aragon is said to have boasted that, exempt by birth and marriage, she had never bathed." Bathing declined in popularity throughout Europe even further during the seventeenth and eighteenth centuries.[11]

According to Siegfried Giedion, during this time the Reformation and Counter-Reformation both considered nakedness to be a sin. People abstained from bathing. As an example, the palace at Versailles, famous for its grandeur, was constructed without consideration to the inclusion of any "drains or privies." This disregard for bathing continued through the beginning of the twentieth century. Giedion writes:

> It may not be superfluous to recall that even in America, which was later to surpass all countries in this sphere, the tub remained a luxury until the twentieth century. American tenements around 1895 had no bathing facilities.[12]

If bathing was uncommon, needless to say, so was swimming. Besides the sinfulness associated with nudity, full body bathing was also associated with death and illness.[13] The war with water came to a slow but sure halt when in 1830, Vincenz Priessnitz introduced to Europe a revolutionary hygienic therapy based on a "back to nature" philosophy. This therapy prescribed the use of nude bathing.[14] Hydropathy, as the water-cure was called, took Europe by storm. According to Charles Panati:

The cure was the 'waters'—mineral, spring, or ocean. By the tens of thousands, Europeans, who for centuries had equated bathing with death, waded, soaked, and paddled in lakes, streams, and surf.[15]

Soon the taboo practice of submerging oneself in water for any reason was demystified. Bathing at resorts, beaches and spas became accepted not only for the therapeutic purposes but also for its leisure and social values. Although the hydropathic bathing espoused by Priessnitz was done in the nude, bathing at beaches took on a different more modest route.

For the most part, men's and women's bathing was segregated. Women dressed in a heavy, high-necked, long-sleeved, bloomer-type bathing suit described as being so heavy that "...waterlogged bathers [drowned when] caught in an undertow." Men's suits were lighter in design.[16]

To insure further privacy, nineteenth century bathers bathed in a device called a "bathing machine." The ritual of bathing began with the woman, fully costumed in her bathing togs, being wheeled into the water in this machine. She would be further hidden from male view by an extension of the machine called the "modesty hood."[17] Needless to say, the time for a bathing beauty contest was not quite yet. Nevertheless, the segregation of men and women at beaches would soon pass, at least in the United States. Banner reports that at several New Jersey resorts men and women were seen to be abandoning this separation. She writes, "At Cape May and Long Branch...women displayed no temerity in bathing with men."[18] The time for the bathing beauty had arrived. Botticelli's Venus, born of the salty brine, was dressed in nothing but splendor. The first bathing beauties would be dressed in outfits more suitable for the land bound than for denizens of the sea.

### The Birth of the Bathing Beauty Contest

According to Frank Deford, the first bathing beauty contest was the Miss United States contest held at Rehoboth Beach, Delaware in 1880.[19] This bathing beauty contest was produced by Joseph H. Dodge, a public official at Rehoboth Beach, in an attempt to attract publicity to the resort. As such, Dodge can be considered the father of bathing beauty contests. At Rehoboth Beach, the contestants were tempted into entering the contest by something more than the honor of being called Miss United States. In this contest, there also was a prize. Ironically, the prize was a bridal trousseau. Supporters of modern day pageants have argued that there is no voyeurism of any sexuality of the vicarious kind involved in pageants. Perhaps the same was true in Rehoboth Beach. The exclusion of married women, at this contest and all pageants since (with the exception of the popular Mrs. America Pageant), indicate that this was not the case. The exclusion of married women might be seen as an indication of married women's status as property. Unmarried women might be considered unexploited territory that can be defiled, if not physically, at least mentally. In its myths, maidenhood has been known to sire saviors, quench the blood thirst of vampires, and appease the hunger of dragons. Whatever its mystique, the hope, power, and promise of maidenhood (and some might say the hopelessness, powerlessness, and dead-end existence of married life) prevailed at Rehoboth Beach.

Marital status was not the only requirement at Rehoboth Beach. The women had to be no more than twenty-five years of age, a minimum of five foot four inches tall, and a maximum of 130 pounds.[20] This was the image of the ideal American woman/girl. She was young, unmarried, tall, and skinny, and undoubtedly, beautiful. Rehoboth Beach and other bathing beauty contests that preceded and followed it, would open yet another door for young, beautiful, unmarried girls to step through. On the other side of that portal the opportunity to attain wealth, fame, and upward mobility awaited. It is important to note that such beauty contests did not offer equal employment opportunity. They were a lucrative career market for pretty girls only. It was official: the beauty contest had made women a house divided by looks. What was once an unspoken truth; what was once covert discrimination based on beauty or the lack thereof was brought to the light, and further was sanctioned by society as an entertainment form—the bathing beauty contest.

### Swimsuits

The popularity of bathing for recreational purposes would be advanced still further by the invention of the swimsuit, a supple, tailored outfit more conducive to the sport of swimming. There is some discrepancy as to the origin of the swimsuit. One version gives credit to the swimmer, Annette Kellerman. According to Banner, Kellerman, a well known professional swimmer, "designed a one-piece swimsuit worn with tights rather than bloomers." Kellerman was arrested for indecent exposure in 1907 while on a promotional campaign to popularize and sell the suit.[21]

Panati offers a different version to the origin of the swimsuit. He bestows the honor of its invention to a Danish immigrant, Carl Jantzen. According to Panati, Jantzen became a partner in Oregon's Portland Knitting Mills in 1883. In 1915, while attempting to create a lighter-weight woolen sweater, he instead developed an elasticized rib-knit stitch.[22] The new material was used for outfits for Portland's Rowing Team. Because of the success and applications of the material the Portland Company soon changed its name to Jantzen Knitting Mills, and, according to Panati, "adopted the slogan: 'The suit that changed bathing to swimming'."[23]

Whether one gives credit to Kellerman or Jantzen or a combination of both for the invention of the swimsuit, the fact remained, by 1920 respectable bathing beauty contests in which contestants wore one-piece bathing suits were a viable entertainment form. It would take the vision of one man to take that form one step further by turning this concept into a unique (and profitable) American creation. That concept was the Beauty Pageant whose birth occurred in 1920, and whose history is told in the following pages.

# Chapter II
# The Frolicking '20s

The Roaring Twenties has gone down in history as the age of Prohibition, the age of flappers and gangsters. It is an age remembered for the raising of hemlines as well as the raising of hell. What it has not been remembered for, however, is the birth of an American art form—the beauty pageant. Nineteen-twenty was the year that, for better or worse, "pageantdom" was officially born. Although there were previous prototypes, it is in 1920 that the pageant genre came into fruition.

### The Fall Frolic of 1920

Credit for the idea of producing the Fall Frolic of 1920 is given by and large to Conrad Eckholm, proprietor of the Monticello Hotel in Atlantic City. Eckholm's proposal was to have the local Business Men's League sponsor a week long event one week after Labor Day to extend the Labor Day Weekend, and thereby benefit the smaller side avenue hotels not on the Boardwalk such as the Monticello. Skeptical at first, the local hotel owners donated $5,916 towards the Frolic. Since most larger hotels still had good business immediately after Labor Day, it was agreed that the Frolic should take place after Labor Day.[1]

The Fall Frolic of 1920 did not feature a beauty contest. It did, however, feature a Rolling Chair Parade which lasted about an hour, and a masked ball on the Steel Pier.[2]

The idea to have a beauty contest as part of the Frolic of 1921 is credited to Harry Finley, an Atlantic City newspaperman. During a meeting of Atlantic City's circulation managers in the winter of 1920, Finley proposed that a "popularity contest" run by newspapers in various cities would increase their circulation. The contest would select the most popular young lady in their individual cities. The prize? A vacation in Atlantic City! This idea was presented to Sam P. Leeds, the President of the Chamber of Commerce who in turn presented the idea to the Hotelmen's Association.[3] The Association agreed to entertain the ladies who would also compete against the other inter-city champions at the 1921 Frolic.

### The Fall Frolic of 1921

Ask anyone today to define the word beauty pageant, and more than likely they will be able to paint a concrete picture using all the assorted colors available through the beauty pageant palette. Ask anyone to do the same in 1921, and the answer would have been quite different if at all answerable. Although the beauty contest concept was already in existence by 1921, and although many of the other elements associated with pageantry also existed in isolation, never before had so many of these diverse forms converged in one common place for one common goal in such a grand scale and scope as in 1921. With no word yet coined to describe the event which was to take place, the press abandoned the official title of Fall Frolic of 1921 opting instead to describe the proceedings with such names as "The Atlantic City Pageant," the "Super-Carnival," or the "Second Annual Pageant."[4]

Whatever the case or for that matter the name, the festivities of 1921 "[swung] off to an auspicious start" at 11:00 a.m. on Wednesday, September 7, 1921 with the arrival of Father Neptune on his seashell barge with his retinue of mermaids.[5] Father Neptune was, in actuality, the eighty year old "famed inventor" of smokeless gun powder, Hudson Maxim.[6] The mermaids were the Inter-City Beauty Contestants: Miss Washington, Margaret Gorman; Miss Philadelphia, Nellie Orr; Miss Camden, Catherine Gearon; Miss Ocean City, Hazel Harris; Miss Pittsburgh, Thelma Matthew; Miss Harrisburg, Emma Pharo.[7]

In keeping with the festive atmosphere, the local press played along with the light-hearted charade by dubbing the Neptune character with such grandiose epithets as "Comber King," "His Bosship of the Briny," "Blue Blood of the Breakers," "Majesty of the Waves," "Sea King," "King Neptune," and others. Whatever the name, the reference was to Hudson Maxim—trident in hand with long white beard and purple robes. Maxim, like subsequent Neptunes, would be the star of the pageant. As Frank Deford writes, "The big attraction...was...Neptune, who was the male attraction for years, until someone had the sense to invent Bert Parks."[8]

According to the itinerary, as Neptune's barge pulled into the beach east of the Million Dollar Pier at 11:00 a.m., train and factory whistles would go off from the different parts of the city announcing the arrival.[9] Reports indicate that Neptune's barge was met not only with the scheduled whistles, but also with the sounds of "[b]ooming deck guns [which] flash[ed] their tribute in a royal salute, sirens, church bells, and other noise makers [which] chorused in a bedlam of greeting...."[10]

In addition to the audible heraldic display, beyond the breakers a flotilla of spectator-filled private yachts in squadron formation added its presence to the visual panorama. Together with the thousands of revelers both on the beach and jamming against the Boardwalk and pier rails, the scene became a total symphony (or cacophony) of sight and sound.[11]

Included in this collage were sixty on-duty life guards and one physician, a Dr. Ruffu.[12] Also a part of the scene were

thousands of sea nymphs in last-minute editions of the 1921 surf apparel—solo attire with nude limbs beneath, that made the lifeguards, pinch-hitting as beach censors, blink, gasp,—and then remember they were officially blind until midnight.[13]

Adding to the picturesque tapestry of sand and surf, Neptune's barge, and the teeming throngs, were the decorated tents and other areas designated for pageant events. On the beach just north of the South Carolina tents, for example, a platform two feet above the sand was erected for dancing. The Virginia Avenue tent designated for judging Friday's Bathers' Revue was covered with flags. From this tent and all the way up the beach to the Garden Pier, "hundreds of national emblems fluttered from ropes."[14] The scene was ready for the arrival of Neptune.

Upon debarkation at the Million Dollar Pier, Neptune was met by Mayor Edward L. Bader who presented him with the key to the city.[15] Upon completion of this opening ceremony, Neptune and his entourage (which included "...his bevy of Beauties—the Inter-City Contest Winners") proceeded on a "slave borne" float passing the estimated 60,000 persons which lined the Boardwalk.[16]

One half-hour after their initial arrival at the Million Dollar Pier, Father Neptune and the eight Inter-City Beauties arrived at Keith's Theatre on the Garden Pier where both a panel of judges and a capacity crowd scrutinized the eight contestants. The ninth Inter-City Contestant, Ethel Charles, Miss Atlantic City, disqualified herself from competition contending that "she was on her home grounds."[17]

After one hour of scrutiny, the judges reached their decision—one that would not be revealed until the following evening at the Governor's Ball on the Steel Pier. The judges were: Howard Chandler Christy, the famed artist, acting as chairman; John Drew, the actor; Gustav Tott, resident manager of the Ritz-Carlton; W. Gordon Fox, Philadelphia artist; and James Fox, an artist with the Atlantic City Press Union.[18]

According to reports, Miss Washington, Margaret Gorman, the eventual winner, was the audience's overall favorite with Nellie Orr, Miss Philadelphia, as the second favorite. Though receiving less approval than Misses Gorman or Orr, the other girls, nevertheless, had their special claque in the audience rooting them on as well.[19]

Upon completion of the judging, the throngs promenaded around the Boardwalk and beaches. Some wore the masks that they would wear in that evening's Frolique.[20] In the interim, between the morning's festivities and the commencement of the Frolique, the revelers were treated to various organized diversions.

Whatever their activity during that time, by 5:00 p.m., many of the residents and visitors had already staked out their observation territories. The crowds, estimated to be between 90 and 100 thousand strong, jammed the Boardwalk, the hotel roofs, the pavilions, and "any other available space between the Steeplechase Pier and Young's Old Pier" to catch a glimpse of the activities. "VIP's" were secluded from the masses in special cordoned-off orchestra and Boardwalk Box Seats. For the most part, these seats were located against the Boardwalk railings. Included among the "elite" were invited guests, chaperons, and pageant officials. The crowds in place, the evening events commenced at approximately 5:30 p.m. with boat races at South Carolina Avenue among the Atlantic City Lifeguards.[21]

At approximately 7:30 p.m., the Night Carnival began in front of Richard's Pavilion on the beach at North Carolina Avenue.[22] The affair began with Neptune and the Inter-City Contestants ascending the huge platform erected on the water's edge near the main tent. On this platform, Neptune, the girls, and the spectators were treated to a two-hour vaudeville show performed by a troupe of juveniles, ranging in age from three to sixteen years old, called Dawson's Dancing Dolls. Their performance began with the illumination from spotlights. While the show was going on, center stage, Neptune and the contestants were constantly in full view of the public. Not only did they play the role of passive spectator, but, in effect, because of their high visibility on the platform, became part of the scenery. At the end of the show the girls were introduced to the crowds, and again, Miss Washington, Margaret Gorman, received an ovation "that could be heard from one end of the beach to the other."[23]

Soon after, a "stupendous illumination" took place. This illumination included search lights throwing their beams from hotel tops and piers to all parts of the beach. Estimated to be worth $35,000, the lights were on loan from the Hog Island Shipyards. In addition to the lights, the "illumination" included a fireworks display consisting of flower pots, skyrockets, a miniature Niagara Falls, boats, and many more designs of various shapes and colors which illuminated the skies for many miles around. As the fireworks burst and fizzled into the Atlantic, booms from gunnery could be heard. In total, the scene resembled "the Battle of Chateau-Thierry...in France." As the pyrotechnic display ended with an appropriately incandescent "good-bye," it was agreed by some attending that the event had been a "huge kaleidoscopic fantasy."[24]

At the close of the above-mentioned events, as a connecting segue to the next activity, Neptune once again boarded his seashell float. Led by a musical group called the Tall Cedars Band, Neptune and his retinue made their way to the Steeplechase Pier's Ballroom for the start of Neptune's Frolique.[25]

The Frolique, planned and arranged by Bill Fennan, manager of the Steeplechase and director of the Night Carnival, in actuality, was a costume ball. Replete with confetti, noise makers, and streamers, it resembled "a great scene usually pictured by motion pictures on a New Year's Eve but, of course, minus the 'pop.' " Being held during Prohibition, the phrase "minus the pop" points out that the affair was without champagne, and, therefore, "dry."[26] This remark stands out blatantly, glaringly and markedly in view of the incongruent and contradicting reality of life in the 1920s Atlantic City. As Vicki Gold Levi, et. al. writes:

With the onset of Prohibition, Atlantic City became one of the East Coast's most notorious seaports. Rum running was a major growth industry, as speed boats—loaded to the gunwales—outraced the Coast Guard in nightly forays.

...[Nevertheless,] [w]hen it came to nabbing bootleggers, Atlantic City law enforcers were often out to lunch.

...While much of the bootlegged liquor was transported elsewhere, a great many bottles were delivered to Atlantic City Night spots.[27]

That spirits flowed freely all around the festivities but never quite mixed with the spirit of pageant gaiety is either a well orchestrated publicist's lie or an amazing story stranger than fiction. What is more amazing, and even so more insulting in its underestimation of the public's gullibility, is the pageant organizers' insistence that its image was (and is) above alcohol or any other contemporary reproach. This attitude would persist through that year's event to present pageants. For example, in the midst of scandal, the pageant has asserted its pristine virginity. In the middle of a gambling town during a high stakes competition, the pageant insists that its contestants must never pull on the one-arm bandits.

Whatever and regardless of the status of the Frolique participant's sobriety, the festivities were reported to be merry indeed. Once again, Neptune sat as a symbolic sentinel overlooking the dance floor. Draped around his throne were the pageant "beauties" who, along with Neptune, took on the hybrid role of passive spectator/scenery. The active participants in the Frolique were the costume contest entrants.[28]

Included in the costume line-up were:

[Contestants dressed up as] Fatima, vamp, Chinamen, school boys and girls, soldiers...gypsies, southern Mammy, Pierot, colonial lady...and a female impersonator.

The judges, headed by Albert J. Feyls, director, included Lewis Rosenthal, Richard Swift, and Alfred Rosenbaum judging the most beautiful male and female costume. David H. Moore, acting as chairman, Milton Seaman, and William J. Hepburn chose the most comical male and female costume. The winners would be announced the following night at the Governor's Ball. The evening's affairs including the Night Carnival and Neptune's Frolique lasted from 7:30 p.m. until midnight.[29]

*Day Two*

Weeks prior to the pageant, Atlantic City and the East were plastered with posters inviting one and all to the event. According to Deford, one press release promised that, " '[t]housands of the most beautiful girls in the land, including stage stars and movie queens, [would] march in bathing review before the judges in the Atlantic City Fall Pageant'. "[30]

As part of the same promotional blitz, advertisements depicting "Sea Nymphs," "Beach Peaches" and "Mermaids," scantily clothed according to the day's standard, appeared daily in the *Atlantic City Daily Press*.[31] These pictures appeared juxtaposed near the entry form, which urged readers to participate in the upcoming Bathers' Revue—a major part of the Second Annual Pageant.

The regulations for the Bathers' Revue were:

1. Entrants will assemble on Garden Pier at New Jersey Ave. and the Beach at 10:00 a.m. on the day of the Revue.

2. The Bathers' Revue will start at 10:30 a.m.

3. The participants will march from the Garden Pier to the Steel Pier, parading up an incline on the Steel Pier through a hall of observation, down an incline to the beach, where they will disassemble.

4. The winners will be selected by chosen judges as entrants pass the reviewing point, and awards will be made the same night at 9 o'clock on the Steel Pier.

5. The judges will act as a Board of Censors.

6. The Board of Censors reserve the right to reject any entry they deem objectionable for any reason.

7. All entrants must POSITIVELY be attired in bathing costume.

8. No person will be permitted to participate unless he or she has sent in a properly filled Entry Blank to the Revue Chairman.[32]

In essence, the rules and regulations were loose and open enough so that any individual or organization could enter. Perhaps the strictest stipulation, other than the requisite entry form, was that all entrants were required to wear bathing attire. Other than that, if an interested individual or group fit into any of the five Revue categories or classifications, he, she, or they could enter. As can be seen in the summary of categories explained below, a category existed for just about everyone.[33]

1. Division No. 1: Organizations—This division was open to all civic, social, athletic, charitable, business organizations. Eligible to participate under this category were groups such as the Red Cross and the Salvation Army; civil servants such as firemen, policemen, and postmen; social and civic clubs such as the Oddfellows and the Elks; fraternities, swim clubs, schools, hotel employees, and so on. To be eligible to enter, however, all members of any group participating in the Revue had to be attired in bathing suits. Prizes to be awarded in this division included a first place Silver Cup, a second place Silver Cup, and Honorable mention for the organization selected as having the most attractive and original appearance.

2. Division No. 2: Children—A first prize Silver Cup, a second prize Annette Kellerman Bathing Outfit, and honorable mention would be awarded to the three cutest participants. Since all entrants in this category must walk the distance of the Revue, eligible children were those from "walking age" to twelve years of age. In this category the strict bathing suit dress code was enforced to include any nurse accompanying a child.

3. Division No. 3: Men—In essence, this was a male beauty contest with a first prize Silver Cup, a second prize bathing suit, and honorable mention being given to men with the best physical appearance in a bathing suit.

4. Division No. 4: Comic—First and second prize Silver Cups and third prize honorable mention would be given to the most "ridiculous, laughable, and unique bathing make ups."

5. Division No. 5: Beauty—This division was divided into two sub-categories: amateur and professional. An explanation follows:

a) Amateur: In this sub-division, the first prize Silver Cup would be awarded to the most beautiful girl in the section. The second prize award would be given to the girl with the prettiest bathing outfit. One girl could not win both awards, however. Honorable mention would be given to a third contestant.

b) Professional: Eligible to enter the Bathers' Revue in this sub-category was any professional actress, motion picture player, and professional swimmer. The first prize Silver Cup would be given to the most beautiful professional. The girl with the prettiest bathing outfit other than the first prize winner would receive second prize—an Annette Kellerman Bathing Outfit. Honorable mention would be given to a third professional beauty.

An interesting if not telling item on Atlantic City's social milieu during the 1921 pageant appears in the regulations. The rules stress that participation in the Professional Beauty Category was limited to females only, *viz.*, no men in drag.

Although scheduled to begin at 10:30 a.m. on Thursday, September 8, 1921, the Bathers' Revue, according to reports, in actuality began at 11:00 a.m. Approximately 100,000 visitors and residents were in attendance, standing in some places twenty feet deep to get glimpses of the Revue. Reports of the event boasted that every city for miles was represented in those crowds. The parade route situated on the sand between the Garden and Steel Piers was not the only area packed with spectators. The Boardwalk, the pavilions, and the piers were also filled to capacity.[34]

Included in the hour long parade was a "mile long line of mermaids" wearing bathing suits that for the period bordered on the scandalous:

The Bathers' Revue was remarkable for the uncensored costumes. One-piece bathing suits were the rule rather than the exception. Nude limbs were in evidence everywhere—and not a guardian of the law molested the fair sea nymphs who pranced about the sands. Every type of beauty was on exhibition, shown to its advantage in the type of sea togs permitted.[35]

Deford speculates that while there might have been a great variety in beauty types, "struggling in hot, loose sand," he doubts whether there were the reported thousands. As for the mile long line, Deford claims that the distance between the Garden and Steel Piers was in actuality 1,300 feet.[36]

Participating in the Revue (besides the "nymphs") were members of the city council including Mayor Bader, all sporting bathing suits. Not to be outdone, the firemen wore red one-piece bathing suits, and the policemen wore all blue bathing suits along with their hats and night sticks. After escorting the mayor and the members of the city council to the Steel Pier, the officers went on duty in what was described as "the most comfortable attire they had ever been permitted to use in the Summer."[37]

Even the usually-robed Neptune donned his swimsuit for the occasion. Neptune, just as in previous events, was once again a key player in the Bathers' Revue. Having strolled behind a sixty-piece band in the Revue, he took his appointed place at the top of a runway leading to the Steel Pier. From his throne he waved his trident, directing the Revue participants to the Marine Hall at the end of the pier where the judges awaited them to pass in review. All winners would be announced that evening at the Governor's Ball.[38]

Besides Neptune, "the sea nymphs," the dignitaries, and the public servants, also participating in the Revue were many different organizations.[39] Among them were members of the Rotary Club, the Girls Hygeia Swimming Club, and the Press-Union Company which chose as its entry a nine foot by six foot copy of the *Atlantic City Daily Press* with a headline and body reporting the very event in which it was at that moment taking part.[40] Also taking part in the festivities was a group of waiters from the Almac Hotel. These waiters appeared bearing a large platter on their shoulders. Reclining in the platter was a "mermaid" in a white one-piece bathing suit. " 'Some chicken' was the chorus."[41]

Many individuals participated in the Revue as well. Among them "vamps dressed in every color of the rainbow" and a couple dressed in a modified Adam and Eve costume.[42] Of particular interest is the list of entrants in the children's division. On this list, one child's name appears inconspicuously along with the names of other children. It is a name familiar to most Americans today—"Milton Berle (professional)." Perhaps by this recognition Berle has the distinction of being the first person to achieve fame from the ranks of *Miss America Pageant* contestants.

Much of the crowd attending the Bathers' Revue that morning stayed for the afternoon's Rolling Chair Parade.[43] The Rolling Chair, an Atlantic City institution was and is a wicker seat big enough to sit either two or three people, depending on the model. Having two wheels in the back and one wheel in the front, the Rolling Chair depends on human "push power" for mobility.[44]

The Rolling Chair appeared for the first time in the Philadelphia Centennial of 1876. A year later they were brought to Atlantic City by a hardware store owner named William Hayday. His intent was to rent them to invalids. Considered a cheap means of transportation, the chairs became popular even among the non-handicapped. Their popularity became the cause of their temporary downfall, however. So many rolling chairs jammed the Boardwalk that officials complained that the Boardwalk was not big enough for them all. A few seasons later, their numbers regulated by law, the Rolling Chairs returned.[45]

By 1921 they were regular Atlantic City fixtures, a part of Atlantic City's personality, a tradition so woven into the Atlantic City tapestry that even with the advent of the electrically powered trams in the 1940s, they still retained, if not their charm, at least their affordability and hence their popularity. It was the Rolling Chair that became not only a part of the celebration that Thursday afternoon in 1921, but in essence the object of the celebration itself.

At approximately 2:30 p.m., Rolling Chairs decorated with flowers and other trimmings rolled down the Boardwalk from Connecticut Avenue to Missouri Avenue; down Missouri Avenue to Atlantic Avenue; up Atlantic Avenue to Rhode Island Avenue where they disbanded.[46]

About five hundred chairs and floats representing organizations, clubs, municipalities, resort industries, firms, and individuals paraded that afternoon. Included in the line-up were Neptune and some "black slaves garbed in skins," the beauty contestants in decorated chairs, and many more. The Rolling Chair awards would be given out with the other prizes that night at the Governor's Ball.[47] Between the end of the Rolling Chair Parade and the Ball, the revelers were treated to a band concert and Community Sing at the Steel Pier. This musicfest began at 7:30 p.m. and ended at 8:00 p.m.[48]

According to the pageant program, the presentation of prizes for the events held during the two day pageant would begin at 8:00 p.m. on the Steel Pier followed by an electrical display at 9:30 p.m., and the Governor's Ball at 10:00 p.m.[49] The pageants' schedule had to be rearranged at the last minute, however, because the awards ceremony lasted until 11:30 p.m. This in part was due to two factors:

[They were]...the long list of prizes to be awarded, and the interruption[s] of the eager crowd to see their beauty win...[In particular] the crowd went wild at the call of Miss Washington...At intervals between the awarding of other prizes, an occasional outburst would be heard for the Capital favorite and Director Endicott would have to introduce her again to quiet the rooters.[50]

Included in the list of prizes were awards for Neptune's Frolique costume contest winners, Bathers' Revue winners, the Inter-City Beauty winners, and the overall beauty winner, recipient of the Golden Mermaid trophy. That girl would be the first Miss America. The results for all the beauty contests held during the two day pageant are as follows:[51]

1. Inter-City Beauty
   a) Amateur: Miss Washington, Margaret Gorman, Watkins Trophy.
   b) Professional: Miss New York, Virginia Lee, Endicott Trophy.
   c) Opposite Type of Beauty [Than Miss Gorman]: Miss Camden,
      Kathryn M. Gearon, $100 in gold.
2. Inter-City Bathers' Revue
   a) First: Miss Washington, Margaret Gorman
   b) Second: Miss Philadelphia, Nellie Orr
   c) Third: Miss Camden, Kathryn Gearon
3. Amateur Bathers' Revue
   a) First: Mazie Saunders
   b) Second: Margaret Price
   c) Third: Margaret Crawford
4. Professional Bathers' Revue
   a) First: Polly Salisbury
   b) Second: Virginia Lee
   c) Third: Sidney Nelson

The winners of the Bathers' Revue from the Inter-City (Margaret Gorman), Amateur (Mazie Saunders), and Professional (Polly Salisbury) categories met head-on for the title of "the most beautiful bathing girl in America." The contest was won on the basis of 50% popular applause and 50% judges' choice. The judges were Howard Chandler Christy, artist, acting as Chairman, New Jersey Governor Edward I. Edwards, Gordon W. Fox, artist, Gustav Tott, hotel manager, and James Fox, artist.[52]

The winners were: Second Runner Up, Polly Salisbury; First Runner Up, Mazie Saunders, and the first Miss America (although not yet called this), Margaret Gorman. As winner, Margaret Gorman was the recipient of the Golden Mermaid Trophy. The Golden Mermaid, a trophy valued at $1,500, would be held one year by the winner. If she or any subsequent winner won the trophy three years in a row, she would get to keep it permanently. During the winner's reign, a bond of $5,000 had to be furnished in order to retain possession of the trophy.[53]

The entire affair ended after 11:30 that evening. Miss Gorman and her parents remained in Atlantic City until Sunday, September 11th. In that interim, she met with reporters and photographers, and as queen of Atlantic City and America, she was toasted at many parties held in her behalf.[54]

For the most part, it was agreed by most of the pageant sponsors, Atlantic City public officials, and the public at large that the pageant had been a huge success. In part, the success of the pageant was measured in capital gains. As Mayor Bader commented:

If the merchants have either stores stocked and no one is here to buy, what good is their stock however fine? We brought the people here by the thousands, and if they wished to purchase anything, the merchants profited.

Other public officials likewise saw the financial merits of the pageant for Atlantic City. Commissioner Bayer, Director of Finance, for example, claimed, "...[that] we will see the eventual good in stimulated railroad travel and hotel patronage."[55]

Whether for the financial boon it brought to Atlantic City or for the enjoyment it brought, most people expressed an interest in renewing the pageant the following year. According to reports, many people suggested that the Bathers' Revue should be extended in length. Others suggested that floats be limited in size because so many top-heavy ones were out of commission early in the parade. Many other suggestions were given.[56] Whether they were taken by those with the authority to put them into effect or not is inconsequential when the overall picture of a community's involvement and input is taken into consideration.

After the event was over, capacity crowds jammed the Colonial Theatre in Atlantic City to catch a glimpse of a film chronicling the spectacular festival in which they had taken active part. The film was held over for three days.[57]

*An Overview of the Miss America Pageants of the 1920s*

The Atlantic City pageants operating from 1922 through 1927 were similar in structure to the 1921 pageant. With each progressive year, however, the pageants increased in number of activities and escalated in the scope of their spectacle. In 1920, the production allotment had been $5,916. In 1921, the city had donated $1,000. In 1922, $12,500 was appropriated. By 1922 the overall production expense had risen from the 1921 cost of $27,000 to $50,000.[58]

Not only was the budget extended but also the duration of the pageant from two days in 1921 to three days in 1922 and 1923, to five days from 1924 on. The number of activities designed for audience involvement increased.[59] Among the added activities were trapshooting contests, hand ball and tennis championships, and ocean swims for men and women. The activities were not the only ones to change. The pageants' beauty contest aspect also changed in form. Among the changes in competition were:

a) the introduction of preliminary eliminations
b) the introduction of the evening gown competition
c) the stipulation that a winner could not return to competition the following year
d) the regulation that only single women could enter the pageant.[60]

In addition, beginning in 1922, the degree of audience participation decreased gradually and progressively. In 1922, the 50% popular vote was taken away. Judges had the only say in the matter.

As the production budgets and activities increased; as the nature and focus of the pageant shifted towards the beauty contest above all other aspects, so did the frenzied, feverish pace of the festival. It was a frivolous Fall Frolic which kept in step and in tune with the spirit of the Roaring Twenties:[61]

A carnival of beauty ran riot on the resort's famous Boardwalk...a rainbow of color that drew upon the splendor of the Orient, the jazz parlors, bathing beaches, and even the circus to form a two mile ribbon that rippled, splashed, and sparkled until the thousands banked solidly on either flank were wild with enthusiasm over the marvelously spectacular picture unfolded before their eyes for two solid hours...There were piquant jazz babies who shook the meanest kind of shoulders, pink-skinned beauties of all types who had come across the continent.[62]

As the passage above suggests, the number of contestants also increased not only in number but from their point of origination. According to Deford, pageant organizer Harry Godshall had seen to it that every major newspaper in every large city in the United States was contacted regarding the pageant. In 1921, the Inter-City Beauty Contest had eight contestants, and, therefore, eight sponsoring newspapers. The 1922 pageant had representatives from fifty seven cities from all over the United States. In 1923, seventy four contestants entered. By 1924, the figure had risen to eighty three contestants.[63] In 1921 the contestant coming the furthest distance was Miss Pittsburgh. In 1922, the contestant claiming that distinction was supposedly from Juneau,

Alaska. Supposedly, because Deford claims that the articles and stories about Miss Alaska arriving in Atlantic City for the 1922 pageant after a journey on dog sled, airplane, train and motor car were fictitious. He proposes that Miss Alaska was in actuality a Mrs. Earl Liederman with no newspaper sponsorship from Alaska or anywhere else. Through newspaper coverage the local Atlantic City pageant was erasing the Atlantic City boundaries and extending its reach across the United States.[64]

As the coverage increased, so did the pageant's popularity. According to reports, during the *Miss America Pageants* of the 1920s, bathhouses were jammed. Beach front amusements and attractions reported heavy business. Traffic on the "pike" was continuous both in the number of motor cars and the flow from day through nightfall. Garages in the area were filled to capacity. According to official tabulations, in 1922, the railroads carried 67,000 people to Atlantic City for the Saturday festivities alone. The Pennsylvania Railroad, which catered to passenger traffic in those days, declared: "As an advertising campaign, the Pageant was a masterpiece, and it couldn't be bought for half a million dollars."[65]

In 1922, over two hundred and fifty thousand people would attend the frolic. In 1923, three hundred thousand spectators were reported in attendance. In 1924, two hundred fifty thousand "watched beauties in Roller Chair Review."[66]

Deford casts a cynical view on the reported numbers. He writes:

...such figures are suspect, since crowd estimates at Atlantic City are always provided by self-serving tourist officials who are almost dutybound to exaggerate.[67]

On the other hand, Adrian Phillips, a retired hotel executive, *Miss America Pageant* past president, current Vice Chairman of the Executive Committee, and active participant in the *Miss America Pageant* since 1922, maintains that the pageants have always had a very large audience. When asked if the audience was predominantly local, Phillips answered, "Of course not. [They're] from all over.... It's a resort audience...plus the contestants' following."[68] Similarly, Lenora S. Slaughter Frapart, *Miss America Pageant* Executive Director from 1935-1967, claims that prior to television coverage the *Miss America Pageant's* audience was from the "Eastern Seaboard primarily, but [also included] several hundred people from [all over] the country including parents, relatives, state, and local directors, etc."[69]

Whatever the case, the crowds were large. Overnight or for the day, they were coming to Atlantic City and spending their dollars. If by creating the *Miss America Pageant* the Hotelmen's Association had hoped for increased Atlantic City business, their wishes had been fulfilled.

The pageant continued in popularity until 1927 when it was suddenly discontinued. Some argue that the pageant was discontinued for financial reasons (including the Depression). Deford discredits this line of reasoning:

For some mysterious reason, the Pageant has always taken pains to promulgate the fiction that it closed down for several years because of the Depression. This was not the case, especially considering that the contest folded early in 1928, almost two years in advance of the Crash...It was abandoned because...the hotel operators soured on it.

They became convinced that the Pageant...gave Atlantic City a bad name, and cost hotels respectable cash-and-carry patrons.[70]

For all its lucrative appeal, the *Miss America Pageant* of the 1920s became the center of criticism. It was condemned by civic and religious organizations for not only being indecent, but also because the contest exploited women for pecuniary purposes, while at the same time corrupting them through rivalry and competition.[71] Whether the pageant sponsors buckled to this outside pressure and bad press, or whether, indeed, it was because of financial considerations is inconsequential. The 1927 *Miss America Pageant* was to be the last—for a while.

### Conclusions

Generically, the pageants of the 1920s, could be classified as pseudo-events, that is, they were non-spontaneous, highly orchestrated, manufactured events which were self-promotional in nature.[72] Initially, the pageant was created to extend Atlantic City's tourist season one week after its traditional end on Labor Day Weekend which, ironically enough, was itself a human construct. As such, the pageant's original aim was not to promote pageantry, beauty, scholarship, or any other such lofty ideal. Its creation was to make money, a point that many pageant aficionados still feel uncomfortable admitting. That the pageant provided a variety of events, diversions, and entertainment was a peripheral amenity to the organizer's aims—business, lucre, and self-promotion.

Not to be seen in a negative light, the pageant concept instead must be lauded as a stroke of entrepreneurial genius. As a business enterprise, the pageant was either cleverly or inadvertently structured to be a big time money-maker. Luring the masses to the events was not the difficult part. The events by design had built-in promotional qualities. Besides the promise of diversion, potential customers were tempted to Atlantic City by the mystique of what proved to be the gimmick with staying power—the Inter City Beauty Contest.

Drawing the people to the resort was not enough, however. The ingenuity in the pageant's schema was that it was also structured to keep the people at the resort once they got there; and further, to keep them there happily spending their money.

With almost a full day's agenda, most events were scheduled either on separate days or on the same day but hours apart. This scheduling favored those living in the local community and the over-night hotel guest rather than the day-tripper. The day-tripper might catch a glimpse of one event and participate in another. To enjoy all of the offerings of the *Miss America Pageant*, however, that day-tripper would either have to wait for hours or travel to Atlantic City the next day. The answer? Stay overnight, of course.

With this goal in mind, events were created which would appeal to wide cross sections of people. Consequently, the events which made up the early *Miss America Pageants* were not only many in number, but also varied in type and appeal. Whatever the form, for the most part, all events were designed to favor audience participation, input, and feedback. Individual community members, organizations, and civic leaders organized, designed, and participated in the different events. In some instances, such as the dances, group swims, and the like, when there was no audience per se, the participants, in effect, became the event.

One might conclude that perhaps this diversity (or ambivalence) in the form of the above events, stems from the *Miss America Pageant* organizers' inexperience in producing such an event, and, hence, the hodgepodge. Whatever the case, the original *Miss America Pageant* organizers were, in fact, pioneers in the creation of a new genre. As such, they should be noted and remembered for their contribution to American popular culture. In borrowing elements germane to pageantry, parades, masquerades, vaudeville, beauty contests, and other spectacles, a new genre, mosaic in form, was created. Whether this form would survive "as-is," vanish, survive by adapting to more established forms, or mutate into another unique form, only history would be able to tell. As of 1927, it appeared that in all likelihood, the Atlantic City pageant, and perhaps pageants in general would cease to exist as a mainstream form of entertainment. Indeed, what city or group would venture to gamble their reputations and fortunes in an enterprise at odds with the moral fiber and ideologies of the American social establishment? Responding to public pressure, in 1927, Atlantic City's golden egg was quietly laid to rest.

# Chapter III
# The Dire Thirties

*The 1933 Miss America Pageant*

In 1933, for unknown reasons, the pageant idea was taken out of "moth-balls" and given another chance at success. If the pageants of the 1920s were roaring, the newly-revived pageant of 1933 was depressing. For one thing, community involvement was minimal as were competition prizes. Miss America 1933, Marian Bergeron remembers:

1933 was a depression year and not the most productive time to become Miss America...[there was] very little [community involvement] in 1933. Survival was more important.[1]

Although the newly-revived pageant of 1933 was under the direction of Armand T. Nichols who had been the director from 1924-1927, it did not get the full backing of the Hotelmen's Association as in the past.[2] The city officials headed by Atlantic City mayor Bacharach, however, still endorsed the pageant. The Mayor, his wife, and Mr. Nichols, presided over the first day's nighttime event, An Evening Dinner Party, which began at 8:30 p.m. on September 5, 1933.[3]

On this first day of the 1933 *Miss America Pageant*, and previous to the Evening Dinner Party, the main event was the arrival of the thirty beauty contestants from 28 states aboard a specially chartered train called the Beauty Special. Unlike Neptune's Arrival in 1921, the contestants' arrival in 1933 was not theatrical in form. It contained none of the staged pageantry or theatricality of the former. Unlike previous pageants, there was no massive water carnival or frolic; there was no Neptune and his court; there were no fireworks, blaring ships' cannons, party boats on the horizon, or greetings from factory whistles.

Instead, the Contestants' Arrival was simply, as the name states, the contestants arriving in town—a non-monumental event minimized further by the small crowd waiting to greet them. What makes this arrival worthy of any attention or further speculation is that it presents a perfect example of how almost anything under the sun can be given importance, relevance, and recognition if properly promoted. What drew attention to this arrival, what separated it from the thousands of other yearly arrivals into Atlantic City, and what made it part of the *Miss America Pageant* events, was its coverage by the press. The arrival was a publicity gimmick. Because it was

26

widely heralded by the press, and because it was given status as part of the pageant by the organizers, it was elevated in stature to a "happening." Consequently, the routine arrival of the contestants became an event—"The Contestants' Arrival on the Beauty Special," a part of the *Miss America Pageant*. By definition, this event was a pseudo-event, or non-event because it was: a) created to be covered by the press, and b) relegated to a position of status merely by its being given status.[4] In this respect, arrivals such as the ones made by presidents, popes, and other luminaries, can and do transcend the ordinary. Through careful orchestration, the non-events are elevated into the realm of mythic importance and relevance. Although the potential was there in 1933, such was not the case in the Contestants' Arrival.

Perhaps because of a lack of preparation; perhaps because of a lack of funds; perhaps because of lack of insight there was no visual or audio theatricality reported at the Contestants' Arrival in 1933. Some might argue that this missed opportunity, so full of promotional possibility, might have been like that proverbial door, which if opened can create institutions or social change; if left closed or half opened, on the other hand, can evaporate into dreams of "could have been." Perhaps if this publicity gimmick had been given more substance, form, and consequence, it might have evolved from non-event to event and further. Instead, it, and by consequence other successive arrivals, were dismissed as irrelevant and seen for what they truly were—arrivals, a.k.a., non-events. If any lesson could have been learned, perhaps it was that a pseudo-event/publicity stunt taken only half way has as much promotional value as no promotion at all.

To paraphrase a colloquial saying: imagine if someone staged your arrival, and nobody came? Though "thousands" is not exactly nobody, compared to the throngs of the 1920s the awaiting masses were sparse indeed.[5] Upon arrival, the contestants were given a whirlwind tour of the city, after which they made a brief appearance on the Boardwalk in front of The Auditorium which, incidentally, was opened in 1929. After this personal appearance, they retreated to the Ritz-Carlton Hotel for some rest. The girls were reported to be extremely tired after the trip.

Part of the reason for this fatigue was the manner in which they had arrived in Atlantic City. In previous pageants, the contestants had been sponsored by local newspapers. The 1933 contestants were sponsored by carnivals and amusement parks. As part of the arrangement, many had to participate in a seven-week vaudeville tour. Maybe it was from their exhaustion or as reported, "it may be the depression," in any case, the 1933 contestants were reported to be more reserved than those in previous pageants.[6]

The Evening Dinner Party held that night in honor of the contestants and thirty visiting newspapers was attended by a crowd estimated to be between 500 and 1,000 strong (or weak by previous standards).[7]

The girls entered the reception held at the Gateway Casino on the arms of uniformed members of the Morris Guard. Previously warned by the Master of Ceremonies, announcer Norman Brokenshire, that their every move was being watched by the judges, the girls walked across the ballroom on the arms of their escorts while those attending the function applauded.[8]

On the second day of the 1933 *Miss America Pageant,* two main events were held. The first was a bathing suit competition held that afternoon.[9] At this competition the attendance was reported to be only a "few." The contestants dressed in bathing suits paced across The Auditorium's stage in front of the judges. Although the judges' scores would not be announced, they would, nonetheless, figure in the final selection tallies. After the Revue, the girls went to see the movie *Ghost Train.*[10]

The evening's events began at approximately 8:30 p.m. with a Fashion Show by 30 "mannequins" at The Auditorium's ballroom stage. This show was staged by Stanley Moore, "famous style creator."[11] At approximately 9:30 p.m., the beauty contestants rolled down the Boardwalk in Rolling Chairs from their hotel for the beginning of the Beauty Ball.[12]

The Ball began with the introduction of the contestants in evening gowns by Garnett Marks. At a signal from the band, the contestants appeared from the wings, stage left. One by one they walked to center stage where they met their "nattily uniformed" escorts who had entered stage right. As the contestant and the escort met, the guardsman bowed, presented the contestant with a rose, and arm in arm promenaded around the stage before the judges. After "all the audience had seen their all," the band struck up a waltz. With everyone joining in the dance, the Beauty Ball had begun. Between 2,000 and 3,000 people attended the function.[13]

The third day of the pageant was the first day of actual competition with preliminary evening gown eliminations scheduled for 8:00 a.m., the Bathers' Revue scheduled for 10:00 a.m. and the evening gown competition scheduled for 9:30 p.m.[14]

Organization was perhaps not a main component in the 1933 pageant. In the previous day's photo session, three girls had forgotten their bathing suits.[15] The Bathers' Revue, like the photo session, was delayed in starting by two hours because one of the judges, Gladys Glad, overslept. To make matters worse, Miss New York State, Florence Meyers, while passing the line of judges screamed and collapsed on the floor because of a bad toothache. Besides the two hour delay and the toothache, The Bathers' Revue progressed if not blandly and uneventfully, at least without any further mishaps.[16]

Unlike the Bathers' Revues of the 1920s, at the 1933 Bathers' Revue there were no teeming throngs. In fact, the revue was held indoors in The Auditorium that year instead of outdoors on the Boardwalk.[17] Heading the Revue was Mayor Bacharach, Dr. David Allman, Chairman of the Pageant Committee, and Director Armand T. Nichols. The parade through the auditorium included twenty girls in white bathing suits riding bicycles, massed flags of the Morris Guards, the St. Louis Letter Carriers, a band from Kentucky, and the Inter-City Beauties on a float. The marchers paraded twice through the two lanes of seats in The Auditorium.[18]

The judging for the contest was done on the stage. The contestants would walk across the stage in competition before a panel of judges which, besides Gladys Glad, included Peter Arno, caricaturist; George White, producer of the "Scandals;" George Beucher and Russell Patterson, New York based artists, and two secret judges. The contestants were judged on personality, carriage, and figure. Prizes were awarded to the professional and amateur beauties in the Revue. No prizes were awarded to the Inter-City Beauties. The professional winner was Miss New York City and the amateur winner was Miss Atlantic City.[19]

The Evening Gown competition actually began at 8:00 a.m. that morning with a process of elimination. It was reported that many girls broke into tears when they were eliminated.[20] The evening competition at The Auditorium was met with a degree of controversy when it was reported that three women would be disqualified because they did not come from the states which they represented. The women in question were Miss Iowa, Miss Idaho, and Miss Illinois.[21]

Approximately three thousand people attended the event which began at 9:30 p.m. The women again paraded in front of the judges at The Auditorium. The winner of the Gold Cup was Miss New York State, Florence Meyers, toothache and all.[22]

The fourth day of the *Miss America Pageant* of 1933 included an ocean swim for residents and tourists in front of The Auditorium at 10:00 a.m., the Rolling Chair Parade at 2:30 p.m., a Fashion Review at 8:30 p.m., and a "Night of Merriment" at 9:30 p.m.[23] Also included in the day's competition agenda for the contestants was a private elimination on The Auditorium stage.[24]

The elimination took place before the seven judges and a "few privileged spectators." The elimination that morning consisted of the thirty Inter-City contestants parading twice in front of the judges in their bathing suits. This process was done in order to narrow the field down to eighteen.[25]

That afternoon, The Auditorium doors swung open to eight thousand spectators attracted there by the scheduled Rolling Chair Parade. In 1933 the *Miss America Pageant* was held indoors, consequently, the "mere" eight thousand could not compare to the hundreds of thousands which lined the Boardwalk in previous years.[26] Like the Bathers' Revue, the Rolling Chair Parade consisting of decorated chairs, beauty contestants, and bands wound up and down the aisles of The Auditorium in review. A feature of the Parade was the announced playing of the *Star Spangled Banner* by the $500,000 pipe organ. The organ in question only played ten bars and then broke down. The day was saved when the mailmen's band "took up the musical burden." The Rolling Chair Parade began at 2:30 p.m.[27] At 8:30 p.m., "an elaborate fashion show" was held as a "warm-up" to the real event of the evening, The Night of Merriment.

The Night of Merriment, a vaudeville song and dance show put on by local talent, began at 9:30 p.m. and played to a crowd of 4,000 people at The Auditorium. The Inter-City Beauty contestants were not involved at all, except for a brief appearance at the end of the show.[28]

The fifth day of pageant activities, Saturday, September 9, 1933, began with an ocean swim in front of The Auditorium at 2:00 p.m. At 2:30 another fashion review was held in The Auditorium. Like the rest of the week's activities, these events existed as peripheral incidentals to the main event—the crowning of Miss America 1933. That would take place that evening at 8:00.[29]

The evening began with the contestants' entrance into The Auditorium. This entrance was similar to the Rolling Chair Parade in that the girls were "rolled" into The Auditorium on decorated chairs by Atlantic City Policemen. The girls rolled up and down the aisles and then up onto the stage.

Upon reaching the stage, the girls were placed in their chairs facing the audience. At this time, the judges were announced to the audience by master of ceremonies, Norman Brokenshire. They were: Gladys Glad, "one-time *Follies* beauty"; George White, *Scandals* producer; Peter Arno, caricaturist; Russell Patterson, Walter Thornton, and Hugh Walters, artists.[30]

The entire group of contestants walked around in a circle in front of the judges. After this, the eighteen semi-finalists selected on Friday were announced. They were: California, Connecticut, Washington D.C., Kentucky, Louisiana, Maine, Massachusetts, Michigan, Mississippi, Missouri, New Jersey, New York, Ohio, Pennsylvania, Virginia, Washington, Wisconsin, and West Virginia.[31]

These eighteen were gradually eliminated. Two women were taken off the stage leaving sixteen, then twelve, and finally four. The finalists were then taken off stage to change into evening gowns. While the girls were changing, organist Arthur Scott Brook entertained the audience on the newly repaired $1,000,000 pipe organ (priced at $500,000 in previous reports).[32]

According to Frank Deford, the following scene occurred next:

Someone brought [Miss Connecticut] her high school gown, and she struggled into it, pulling it over her bathing suit. She did not know quite what was going on...Miss New York State and Miss California, were also backstage changing. 'Nobody told me I was Miss America until they put the banner on me,' [Miss Connecticut] Marian [Bergeron] says.[33]

The women returned to the stage in their evening gowns on the arm of an escort, a Morris Guardsman. Marian Bergeron, Miss Connecticut, now Miss America 1933, "walked into the lights, with two little pages holding her robe...Armand T. Nichols, crowned her placing the diadem at a rakish tilt." The program ended at 10:00 p.m.[34]

Among the prizes Miss America 1933 received were a Ford automobile, a wrist watch, and a trip to Bermuda. Reminiscing about her prizes and her reign, Marian Bergeron states:

Being a Miss America in 1933 gave you a better sense as to the pulse of the people in general. Prizes were not monetary, and of course, no scholarship money. Everyone shared and gave of themselves. It was a beautiful rewarding experience.[35]

Although it might have been a beautiful experience for Miss America 1933, for the producers and organizers it was not. Armand T. Nichols complained of the lack of cooperation from everyone especially the Chamber of Commerce. Mayor Bacharach went on record as saying that no money had been made on the pageant. Whatever the case, the pageant was "discontinued after one year and a financial fiasco."[36]

### An Overview of the Miss America Pageant in the Mid to Late 1930s

In 1934, no contest was held in Atlantic City, although an "American Queen of Beauty" was chosen in Madison Square Garden. The winner was Helen Mack of South Ozone Park, New York.[37] In 1935, the idea to revive the pageant was again contemplated.

Eddie Corcoran, Promotion Manager and Publicity Director for the Steel Pier, proposed the idea to his employer, Frank P. Gravatt. The event had been a major financial and promotional success during the 1920s. Corcoran believed that by re-organizing the pageant based on sound business principles, it could once again become a great Atlantic City civic event. In addition, if run correctly, its promotional benefits could be a great boon to Atlantic City business—not to mention Gravatt's Steel Pier Amusement Palace. The Variety Club of Philadelphia, to which both Corcoran and Gravatt belonged, volunteered to establish contests in communities where Variety Clubs were located.[38]

The new contest would be called *The Showman's Variety Jubilee*.[39] The organizers agreed to finance and promote the contests, to stage the Pageant on the Steel Pier, to finance the Boardwalk Parade, and to provide hotel accommodations and entertainment for the contestants. Fifty-two contestants representing eleven states and forty-one cities would enter the 1935 *Showman's Jubilee*.[40]

To coordinate the new project, Corcoran hired Lenora Slaughter, a member of the St. Petersburg Florida Chamber of Commerce staff.[41] An article featuring Slaughter's coordination of the "Festival of States Parade" in St. Petersburg, had been disseminated nationally through the Associated Press. The article was read by Corcoran. He contacted Al Lang, a member of the St. Petersburg Chamber of Commerce, to ask if Slaughter could be borrowed for six weeks. The proposition was accepted. Lenora Slaughter would be "loaned" to Atlantic City for six weeks. Slaughter was given a $1,000 stipend by Lang.[42]

The 1935 *Miss America Pageant* coordinated by Lenora Slaughter differed from previous pageants in several respects. In 1935, after eight years of dormancy, the Boardwalk Parade would be "resurrected." Over fifty-four floats and over thirty decorated cars would roll down the Boardwalk on the afternoon of Friday, September 6, 1935. The parade would be led by

King Neptune, a.k.a. Captain Thaddeus Cowden, and witnessed by over 350,000 spectators.[43]

The 1935 *Miss America Pageant* would also be the first to conduct three nights of official preliminaries in front of a "small and curious audience[s]" at the Marine Ballroom on the Steel Pier.[44] A winner and runner-ups were chosen in the evening gown and bathing suit competitions.

The winner of Wednesday night's preliminary Evening Gown competition was Miss California, Virginia Hope Donham. First runner-up was Miss Philadelphia, Jean Kathryn McCool; second runner-up was Miss Baltimore, Frances Stine; honorable mention went to Miss Pittsburgh, Henrietta Leaver; Miss New York, Vera Haal; also Miss Des Moines, Connie Rosalie Rosefield. Three thousand people attended.[45]

The Bathing Suit competition was held on Thursday evening. The winner of the Bathing Suit competition, "America's Most Beautiful Bathing Girl," was Miss New York, Vera Haal. The first runner-up was Miss Connecticut, Margaretta Kling; the second runner-up was Miss Baltimore, Frances Stine; the third runner-up was Miss Philadelphia, Jean Kathryn McCool; the fourth runner-up was Miss California, Virginia Donham.[46]

The 1935 pageant would also be the first *Miss America Pageant* to include a talent competition. Although not required to, approximately half of the contestants entered. The talent competition was held on Friday evening from 9:00 p.m. to 10:30 p.m. No prize was given for talent.[47]

The 1935 *Showman's Variety Jubilee* would also have the distinction of being the first *Miss America Pageant* to have an age requirement of eighteen years of age for participation eligibility.[48] The hostess committee was also established in 1935. This committee was made up of Atlantic City women who would chaperon the contestants from 9:00 a.m. until midnight every day of pageant week.[49]

Over 5,000 people stood throughout the three-hour competition held at the Ballroom. After the show, the winner, Miss Pittsburgh, Henrietta Leaver, sang and danced before a crowd of 15,000 people on the Steel Pier. According to the *New York Times*, "In a speech of acceptance [Leaver] told the audience that she had sung and danced only once before in public."[50]

The 1935 *Miss America Pageant* was a critical success. Moreover, the "profits" of the 1935 *Miss America Pageant* reduced the former pageant deficit by $5,000.[51] Because of the 1935 *Miss America Pageant's* success, Lenora Slaughter was asked to return the following year to organize the 1936 *Miss America Pageant*. She was offered a salary of $3,000.[52] She accepted the position as Eddie Corcoran's second in command, and took over temporarily when Corcoran died that Spring. George Tyson from Pittsburgh was brought in to supervise as Executive Director. Lenora Slaughter was made Associate Director under Tyson.[53] That same year the *Showman's Variety Jubilee* was incorporated as a non-profit civic corporation of the State of New Jersey.[54]

*Changes in the Miss America Pageant Between 1936 and 1939*

The pageant, under the leadership of Lenora Slaughter, underwent many changes in policy, format, and structure between 1936 and 1937. Some of these changes are as follows:

| | |
|---|---|
| 1936 | Box seats were available to contestants' parents and "important dignitaries." Everyone else stood.[55] |
| 1937 | The rule that five contestants from each of the preliminaries would be chosen to compete in the Saturday Finals was instituted.[56] |
| | A rule banning all contestants from night clubs, bars, inns, and taverns was also created. |
| | A curfew of 1:00 a.m. also went into effect that year.[57] |
| | Contestants could not be seen with or talk to *any* man during pageant week. [emphasis added] Taxis were to be used only for necessary transportation. This rule went into effect because of an incident happening in 1937. In 1937 the pageant remained without a Miss America. Miss America 1937, Bette Cooper, had run away with her chauffeur on the evening that she was crowned.[58] |
| 1938 | The talent competition became a required element of competition. |
| | All contestants were required to compete under the title of a key city, a state, or a geographical region, *i.e.*, no amusement park or carnival affiliation. |
| | Contestants had to be between the ages of eighteen and twenty eight on the opening day of the pageant. |
| | Contestants were limited to single girls, *i.e.*, never married, never divorced, or having a marriage annulled.[59] |
| 1939 | The actual format of the *Miss America Pageant* was changed. For the preliminary competitions, one third of the contestants competed in evening gown, bathing suit, and talent in each of three preliminaries. "Thus giving the girls more time for talent rehearsal." |
| | The Miss Congeniality Award was first given. |
| | The development of Western State Pageants was inaugurated.[60] |

By the end of the 1930s the *Miss America Pageant* was pretty well set in its format and rules. Moreover, its existence, if not its fame, was reaching all corners of the United States. Nineteen thirty-eight's winner, Marilyn Meseke, was seen by approximately 112 million movie-goers in *Movietone News*[reel] as she was being crowned.[61] The pageant's popularity would increase during the 1940s—the war years.

# Chapter IV
# The War Years

## The Early 1940s

Nineteen forty was a year of change for the *Miss America Pageant*. For starters, it was in 1940 that the *Showman's Variety Jubilee* officially became known as the *Miss America Pageant*.[1] The pageant was incorporated as a non-profit civic corporation with a board of directors made up of eighteen business leaders. These leaders would be selected at an annual membership meeting. This meeting would be attended by representatives and officers from Atlantic City social, civic, and cultural organizations.[2]

In 1940 the pageant also moved from the Steel Pier into the newly constructed Convention Hall.[3] According to Frank Deford, Lenora Slaughter wrote, "Promptly at 8:30, the huge curtains rose on the great stage, and a veritable fairyland of beautiful flowers and lovely girls came into view." A reported 25,000 people attended that 1940 pageant.[4]

Besides the move to Convention Hall, other changes were initiated in the *Miss America Pageant* in 1941:

1. The panel of judges was limited to a minimum of nine and a maximum of eleven.
2. Judges were required to be present at all three preliminaries.
3. A breakfast meeting with the judges would be arranged for the contestants so that the finalists did not have to be interviewed in the judges' box.
4. No losing contestant could return to Atlantic City a second time to vie for the title of Miss America.[5]

The above rules were brought to fruition based on *Miss America Pageant* Board decisions. A catalyst of change outside the realm of the *Miss America Pageant* or media control occurred in 1941—World War II. Because of the hardships of the War, the pageant budget was cut from $50,000 to $16,000.[6] To complicate matters, Convention Hall was taken over by the armed forces. The pageant was without "a home." Madison Square Garden, which according to Deford, "would book the Amazon River if it could figure a way to pirate it out of Brazil," offered $10,000 to produce the pageant— at the Garden.[7] Pageant officials were opposed to this idea since it went against the original intent of the pageant, *i.e.*, to extend *Atlantic City's* summer season past Labor Day. Rather than move to New York, it would behoove the Pageant and all involved with it to cancel it altogether until after the war.[8]

According to Susan Dworkin, Lenora Slaughter came to the rescue:

The local manager didn't want to rent [the Warner Theatre] to us...[b]ut I went right to the top. Rose Coyle, Miss America, 1936, had married Henry Schlesinger, who was one of the important men in the Warner chain...I told him that the manager in Atlantic City wouldn't rent to us...Schlesinger got hold of the big boys in Hollywood and called me and said, 'You've got it, dear.' It was a great break for Atlantic City and a great break for me....

George Tyson [*Miss America Pageant* Director]...was fired, and I got his job.[9]

The pageant was moved to the Warner Theatre for the duration of the War.

### The 1943 Miss America Pageant

In 1943, Atlantic City once again considered cancelling the *Miss America Pageant* for the duration of the war. Objections were raised by businesses depending on Miss America bookings and endorsements. State and local pageants which had invested both time and money in preparation for the pageant, likewise, objected.

An additional factor prompted the *Miss America Pageant* organizers to re-consider cancellation. As in 1941, Madison Square Garden threatened that if the pageant were cancelled, it would take it over. *Miss America Pageant* organizers decided that the pageant must and would go on—in Atlantic City.[10]

The *Miss America Pageant* officials took their proposals to the federal War Finance Department (WFD) which had a say as to which events of its kind could take place during the War. After careful consideration, the 1943 *Miss America Pageant* was given a "green light" by the government with the stipulation that no activity interfere with the war programs.[11]

A great part of the reason for allowing the continuation of the pageant was purely for public relations purposes. The WFD recognized the *Miss America Pageant's* endorsement potential in the selling of war bonds. According to Lenora Slaughter:

The War Finance Department knew we could do a good job of selling bonds.... They agreed to pay [$2,500] if I would chaperon Miss America on a trip around America selling war bonds in 1943.[12]

Even with the government's backing, efforts to produce the 1943 *Miss America Pageant* were laced with obstacles. Because of the War, there was a shortage of materials and workmen for the construction of floats. Consequently, the traditional Boardwalk Parade had to be cancelled that year.[13]

Financing the pageant also posed a difficult problem. The proposed production budget for the pageant was $22,500. Since the bulk of this budget would come directly from ticket sales, an all-out effort was made by Atlantic City civic organizations for the promotion and sale of tickets.[14] Tickets for the *Miss America Pageant* events held at the 4,000-seat Warner Theatre ranged in price from $.55 to $2.20 for general admission. The first one thousand orchestra seats sold for $7.50 for a four-nights' season ticket.[15] The sales campaign worked. Advanced sales for the pageant were reported to be heavy. In addition, Lever Bros. offered $5,000 in aid based on the agreement that Miss America would help the war effort by going on a bond selling tour.[16] The budget considerations were met. The pageant, although produced on a "shoestring," was ready to begin.

Preliminaries

The 1943 *Miss America Pageant*, dubbed by the *New York Times* as *The Miss America Beauty, Health, and Talent Pageant*, began on Wednesday, September 8, 1943.[17] It was produced that year by Hollywood producer Oscar Meinhardt and staged by J. Howard Buzby. The pageant, consisting of three nights of preliminary competitions, would culminate on Saturday night with the crowning of the new Miss America.[18]

The preliminary contests held on Wednesday, Thursday, and Friday night were identical in all production aspects. The difference in each night's program was in the competition portions of the pageant. To select the sixteenth Miss America, the thirty-three contestants were divided into three competition groups for the preliminary judging. Each night, one third of the contestants would be judged in evening gown, one third in bathing suits, and one third in talent. By the end of Friday night's competitions, each contestant would have appeared in each of the three divisions of the contest. A winner in the bathing suit and talent categories would be announced at the end of each program. No winner would be announced in the evening gown competition.[19]

The preliminary night show was "patriotic" in theme, beginning with a "Stage Door Canteen" number. This number featured vocalist Seaman First Class Jimmy Conlon of the United States Coast Guard Training Station. At the beginning of the show, Master of Ceremonies Bob Russell, by way of "greeting" Conlon at the "Stage Door," introduced him to the audience. Russell was accompanied at the time by Specialist Third Class William Dwyer, and Coxswain Henry Ford of the Coast Guard. Next, each of the thirty–three contestants appeared at the "Stage Door" and was introduced to the service men and the audience.[20]

The introduction of the contestants ushered in the next production number, "The Parade of Allies." For this number, each contestant appeared dressed in the native costume of a member of the United Nations. Carrying that nation's flag, each contestant paraded around the runway constructed around the orchestra pit. Having finished her promenade around the runway, each contestant took her place on the raised platform built on the stage.[21]

The procession opened with South American countries and ended with girls representing China, Russia, and Great Britain. Jo-Carroll Dennison, Miss America 1942, entered representing the United States dressed as "The Goddess of Liberty." Dennison took her place on the throne overlooking the set. She was flanked by women dressed as WAC, WAVE, SPARS, Marine,

AWVS, Canteen Worker, Red Cross, and defense workers. Having reached her throne, Dennison, the contestants, and everyone else on stage led the audience in the singing of "The Star Spangled Banner."[22]

The introductions complete, the competition portion of the *Miss America Pageant*, bathing suit, evening gown, and talent were ready to begin. In order to facilitate costume and scene changes, however, musical song and dance numbers by professional acts, Bob Russell, and Jo-Carroll Dennison were sandwiched between each competition segment. In one segment, Russell sang a medley of songs from *Oklahoma*. Dennison gave an encore performance of her 1942 *Miss America Pageant* show stopper "Deep in the Heart of Texas" during another segment. Dancer Peggy Craft performed a tap routine during still another of the interludes.[23]

The first competitive event was the bathing suit competition. In this competition, the contestants made their appearance framed against a silver panel at the edge of the stage that "silhouetted the shapeliness of their trim black suits." Each contestant circled the runway once, and then took her place on the elevated platform.[24]

The evening gown competition followed. Each contestant appeared through the opening in a huge green vase. The set piece on stage was topped with a cluster of artificial red roses erected on stage.[25] The gowns varied in style and color with the only similarity being the rosette each woman wore identifying her by title, *e.g.*, Miss New York or Miss New York City.

The final competition segment was the talent competition. Though the range in talent varied, the type of entry, for the most part, did not. Most of the selections were popular songs.[26] One exception in talent was offered by Miss Cincinnati, Joan Hyldoft who "ice skated" on the bare wooden boards of the Warner Theatre's stage on Friday night. Knowing that "real" ice would not be available in Atlantic City for skating purposes, Hyldoft was prepared to skate on "muck ice," a chemical preparation spread like putty on flat boards. Since "muck ice" contained ingredients classified as "trade secret . . . war vital chemicals," it could not be easily obtained. Hyldoft's managers found and purchased perhaps "the last bit of muck ice in the country." The muck ice arrived in Atlantic City where an eight foot by twelve foot rink was manufactured to hold it. This make-shift rink was stored in a lot near the Warner Theatre. Needless to say, after days on the lot with the sun beating on it, the muck ice turned into a syrupy mixture:

Miss Cincinnati, undismayed, tried to skate on [the melted muck ice] yesterday morning. Then she found that the heat had done something to its surface. She stuck fast as though on a huge sheet of flypaper.[27]

Relentless, Hyldoft went on, twirling, jumping, and spinning her way to victory in that night's talent competition on the bare floor.[28] Other winners of the preliminary competitions including Hyldoft were:

Wednesday

Wednesday
    Miss Boston, Helena Frances Mack (Bathing Suit) (Tie)
    Miss Western Pennsylvania, Emma Hammermeister (Bathing Suit) (Tie)
    Miss California, Jean Bartel (Talent)
Thursday
    Miss Washington DC, Dixie Lou Rafter (Bathing Suit)
    Miss Boston, Helena Mack (Talent)
Friday
    Miss California, Jean Bartel (Bathing Suit)
    Miss Cincinnati, Joan Hyldoft (Talent)

Judges for the competitions were:

1. Vincent Trotta, Art Director, Paramount Pictures
2. Hap Hadley, Commercial Artist
3. Conrad Thibault, Radio and Concert Singer
4. W. W. Forster, editor, Pittsburgh Press
5. Russell Patterson, Magazine Illustrator
6. Horace Schmidlapp, financial backer of *Oklahoma*
7. John Robert Powers, modeling executive
8. Martin Banner, author of "Winnie Winkle" cartoon strip
9. Alex Raymond, creator of Flash Gordon
10. Prunella Wood, fashion stylist
11. Henry Conover, modeling executive

Approximately four thousand spectators saw the show each night of preliminaries.[29]

### Finals

According to reports, an overflow crowd of nearly five thousand packed the Warner Theatre for the final night of competitions on Saturday night, September 11, 1943. The program for the Finals was identical to the preliminary night competitions with a few variations.[30]

Just as in the preliminaries, the Finals began with the Miss America Canteen number. As before, Bob Russell introduced each of the thirty-three contestants. Each circled the ramp, then entered the "Stage Door Canteen." After all of the girls had been introduced, the curtain rose to reveal the full stage with all of the contestants blocked throughout the stage.[31]

Next, Bob Russell introduced Miss Atlantic City, Barbara Lu Dora Jones. Miss Atlantic City, as in the past, acted only as official hostess, and as such extended a few words of greeting to the contestants and to the audience. After Miss Atlantic City's welcome, Jo-Carroll Dennison, Miss America 1942, was introduced to the audience. She walked around the ramp to thunderous applause and then took her place on the throne placed center stage, high above the contestants.[32]

The competition segment of the show followed. That night, however, only the ten contestants with the most accumulated points in the preliminary competitions would compete. Bob Russell announced the names of the top ten finalists. They were Miss California, Miss Boston, Miss Florida, Miss Washington DC, Miss Arkansas, Miss New York City, Miss New Jersey, Miss Minnesota, and Miss Western Pennsylvania.[33]

The evening gown competition followed. Each of the top ten contestants entered through a carefully concealed partition in the huge green vase decorating the stage. Each circled the ramp once, then took her place in a straight line opposite the judges' box for close-up scrutiny. The ballots were collected and turned over to Colonel Harrison Cook as the contestants left the stage to a "prolonged applause." Just as in the preliminaries, between each competition segment, the audience was entertained. The entertainment numbers included song-and-dance numbers by Bob Russell and Jo-Carroll Dennison.[34]

For the bathing suit competition, the contestants appeared upstage against a silver drop. They descended a short flight of stairs, circled the ramp, they lined up in front of the judges. The talent competition followed. In this competition, the women repeated their preliminary night performances. The numbers for the most part were popular songs with the exception of two baton twirling acts.[35]

While the judges made their decisions, the audience was entertained by the Coast Guard Training Station Orchestra, led by Radioman Second Class Warren Davis, a former trumpeter with George Olsen's Orchestra. The numbers included the Coast Guard Anthem, "Semper Paratus," "Paper Doll," and "All or Nothing at All." Davis next introduced a song written especially for the pageant titled, " 'Tis the Girls." The band concluded with "Gobs of Love."

The selection of Miss America 1943, the second wartime Miss America, followed. The announcement was made by Bob Russell: the fourth runner-up, Miss Washington, DC, Dixie Lou Rafter; the third runner-up, Miss New York City, Milena Mae Miller; the second runner-up, Miss Boston, Helena Frances Mack; the first runner-up, Miss Florida, Muriel Elizabeth Smith. The new Miss America was Miss California, Jean Bartel, a nineteen-year-old sophomore at the University of California at Los Angeles (UCLA). Her prize was "a huge Miss America Trophy."[36]

As per agreement, the new Miss America embarked on a three month bond-selling tour to fifty-three cities in the United States. Over one million dollars in Series E bonds were sold.[37] More than just being a successful patriotic endeavor, the tour accidentally brought about one of the major innovations in the *Miss America Pageant*—the idea for scholarship awards.

When the tour reached Minneapolis, the Kappa Kappa Gamma sorority at the University of Minnesota promptly invited sorority sister Jean Bartel and her traveling companion, Lenora Slaughter, to afternoon tea. Exactly who came up with the idea that the *Miss America Pageant* should provide scholarship money for its winners is subject to debate.[38] Regardless, the idea became an obsession to Slaughter, who wished to elevate the contest's image:

> I left Minnesota with the determination to give a scholarship to Miss America....
> In 1943, when I got my board to approve [to give]...a scholarship to Miss America, I
> had the Second World War to contend with. So it took me until 1944 to raise the money.
> I was fighting a battle to get a thousand dollars from [each] of five companies.[39]

Slaughter got the money from Catalina Swimsuits, Joseph Bancroft and Sons Company, Fitch Shampoo, Harvel Watches, and the Sandy Valley Grocery Company. In 1945 the first pageant scholarship would be given. Since 1945 the scholarship awards at the local, state, and national levels have grown. According to Lenora Slaughter:

> Today [1987] the pageant is recognized as the greatest scholarship program for girls in
> the world...[t]he Miss America Pageant and the America's Junior Miss Pageant[s] are
> the only two national pageants operated as non-profit civic organizations. All others are
> commercially sponsored for monetary gain...over 2,500 civic leaders serve...year
> round...on the many committees associated with the pageant.[40]

Nineteen forty-five was a landmark year for the pageant for other reasons, as well. With the war finally over, the Boardwalk parade was reinstated. It would be a victory parade. As Bess Myerson, Miss New York City, rolled down the Boardwalk in the Victory Parade, she little realized that she would make pageant history. She would be the first Jewish Miss America; she would be the first recipient of the Miss America Scholarship; she would be the first Miss America to be crowned after the declaration of peace.[41]

### Changes in the Miss America Pageant Between 1945 and 1952

Other than the above, other changes occurred in the rules or structure of the *Miss America Pageant* after 1945:

1946    The phrase bathing suit was replaced by the word swimsuit in pageant vocabulary.

1947    The contestants would be judged in a fourth category, Intellect and Personality, based on interview questions.

1948    Miss America 1948, BeBe Shoppe's, coronation was held with the winner dressed in an evening gown rather than a swimsuit.

1949    Key city representation was eliminated with the exception of New York, Chicago, Philadelphia, Washington DC, Canada, and the territories.

        Animals were banned from use in the talent competition after Miss Montana 1949, Carol Fraser, and her horse almost fell into the orchestra pit during the 1949 pageant.[42]

Although affected by the War, the pageant, rather than waning, reached new heights in popularity. By the decade's end the pageant's format and identity was well established. However, the fifties were just around the corner and waiting there was a power perhaps stronger than war—television.

# Chapter V
# 1953: (Still) Live from Atlantic City

*Miss America in the 1950s*

The early fifties saw the *Miss America Pageant* finally ending its thirty year struggle to solidify not only its identity but also that of its standard bearer, Miss America. The "moral crusade" waged from within by Lenora Slaughter and Miss America 1947, BeBe Shoppe among others, was over, and Miss America clearly had won.

The birth of the fifties saw the Pageant emerging from its growth years of the forties as a mature form ready to take its place with established American institutions. It seems appropriate then, that the pageants of the fifties were literally costumed and styled like debutante balls. The pageant of the early fifties could answer with certainty the questions: "Who are we and what do we represent?" By 1953, the year before television's intrusion, the pageant could proudly hail that it was set in its ways. The identity crisis of an adolescent pageant had been replaced by a pageant assured of its stride with mainstream American society. The pageant's credibility was one that was as strong as the foundation upon which Convention Hall was built. Cynics, on the other hand, could argue that the Pageant's image was, in fact, merely a castle made of Atlantic City sand, ready to be washed away by social tides.

Taking itself and its pristine image quite seriously by the beginning of the fifties, the *Miss America Pageant* seemed to have come a long way from the socially disdained cattle calls of the twenties to the respectability of social acceptance. In keeping with this image, the contestants were, therefore, to be considered singers, scholars, speakers and anything else but sex objects. The world might think of the pageant as just a beauty contest, but the pageant folks, perhaps enveloped in myopic delusion, thought of themselves as everything else but. As such, in 1951, Yolande Betbeze's, Miss America 1951, refused to pose before the cameras in a swimsuit. She was a singer, not a beauty queen, after all. This unbending posture instigated the rift between the Pageant and Catalina Swim Wear, who thought differently. When the pageant organizers refused to yield to Catalina's demands, the bathing suit company broke off its sponsorship with the *Miss America Pageant*, allied itself with Universal International, and formed the Miss Universe Pageant, a pageant which makes no bones as to what it really is.[1]

41

Some argue that this preoccupation with propriety, this insistence on promulgating an antebellum ethos, this casting of pageant women in the roles of belles from days gone by was merely in keeping with the times and the role of women in that time. Therefore, the pageant was merely a mirror of 1950s society. Others would argue that this obsessive compulsion with sanitizing the pageant, this phobia against anything that even insinuated s-e-x, emerged instead from the personal politics and mind set of pageant organizers, people who were more concerned with the image of their bread and butter than with anyone's individual reputation. Altruistic or opportunistic, whatever the case, in 1951 still another regulation was passed concerning the sexual proclivities of pageant contestants. This rule forbade Miss America to marry during her reign. This rule came about because of the aborted marriage of Miss America 1949, Jacques Mercer, during her reign. Mercer insisted that this regulation be put into effect after her "teen-age nuptial folly ended."[2] Thinking this prudent, the pageant people obliged.

Other changes occurring in the early 1950s included an odd tradition which, in effect, attempted to tamper with time. This practice has been called the "post-dating of Miss America." Until 1949, Miss America's title included the year in which she was crowned, *i.e.*, Miss America 1945 was crowned in September of 1945. The bulk of Miss America's reign lay between January and September of the year following the coronation. Starting with 1950, the winner would be recognized by the year of her "reign," *ergo*, post-dating. Although there was a 1950 *Miss America Pageant*, there was no Miss America 1950. The winner crowned in 1950 was called Miss America 1951. All subsequent winners would follow the same classification procedure.[3]

One final change before television's introduction was instituted in 1951: the fifteen semi-finalists were narrowed down to ten.[4] By 1953, the pageant was ready to declare to the world via television that it was what it was and that was what America was too. Before that could be done, though, 1953 would first serve as a final dress rehearsal in front of a home audience.

### *The 1953 Miss America Pageant*

The 1953 *Miss America Pageant* ran for five nights. The schedule of events began with the "American Beauty [Boardwalk] Parade" on Tuesday, September 8, 1953. The festivities continued with preliminaries on Wednesday, Thursday, and Friday nights. The Finals were held on Saturday night with the coronation of Miss America 1954. The competition included four phases: evening gown for poise, grace, and beauty; swimsuit for beauty of face and figure; talent; personality and intellect. Personality and intellect were judged at breakfast meetings with the judges.[5]

Changes in the *Miss America Pageant's* organization that year included the "in-house" publication of the *Souvenir Program Book*. This program book had three purposes:

One, To give you pictures and interesting data on each of our contestants for the Miss America Title.

Two, To give you a pictorial souvenir of Atlantic City and...

Three, To take you behind the scenes and introduce you to some of our great institutions and the civic leaders who have contributed to the growth of Atlantic City as well as the Miss America Pageant.[6]

In 1953, for the first time, the *Miss America Pageant* organization also published and disseminated a manual to local and state pageant directors with suggestions on how to conduct a successful pageant. Other changes in 1953 required that all contestants be graduates of an accredited high school; the contestants also had to present a three-minute talent routine; no contestant would be allowed to speak to any man including her father during pageant week.[7] The legitimization of the pageant's image continued.

### The Boardwalk Parade

The "American Beauty Parade" got underway at 3:00 p.m. on September 8, 1953 as scheduled. The parade moved down the Boardwalk from New Jersey Avenue to Hartford Avenue. A review stand was set up at Convention Hall for judges and Pageant officials.[8] According to reports:

the American Beauty Parade...followed the usual script, even to the perfect weather...thousands upon thousands of spectators...jammed every inch of available space along the Boardwalk from end to end.[9]

The parade began with the appearance of the Grand Marshal, Eddie Fisher, "current song sensation," riding in a convertible car. Fisher's car was followed by the eighty-five-piece Philadelphia Police Band along with patrolmen from Atlantic City. Next to appear was a "crack detachment" of Marines with representatives from bases throughout the east coast. These Marines acted as Color Guard. Another group of Marines acted as Honor Guard for Miss America 1953's float.[10] This float was shaped in the form of a giant crown with a smaller crown in the forefront. Miss America 1953, Neva Jane Langley, rode atop this float wearing a rhinestone-spangled gown. She carried her scepter and waved to the crowds. Miss America's float was followed by Miss Atlantic City's float. As in previous years, Miss Atlantic City acted in a non-competing role as pageant hostess. After Miss Atlantic City, all fifty-two contestants appeared. Each rode in either a Nash Rambler float or a float provided by a state or commercial organization. Beginning in alphabetical order with Miss Alabama all contestants were seen wearing evening gowns of assorted style and color. Included in the line-up were representatives from Canada and Puerto Rico.[11]

The Parade was visually and aurally spectacular. Reports indicate that the gowns, the floats, and the pretty girls added color to the event. The floats were elaborate. One float was designed in the shape of a castle; another in the shape of a lobster; still others were decorated with flying fish, giant toys, lighthouses, forests, and much more. Music was supplied in constant flow from string bands, drum and bugle corps, high school and community bands, and a Mummers Band. The parade lasted about three hours. Float winners in four divisions—Sweepstakes Trophy, Hotel Division, Commercial Division, and State Division—were announced the following day.[12]

*Preliminaries*

The preliminary contests prior to the Saturday night Finals would be held each night for three consecutive nights at 8:30 p.m. The first preliminary show would begin on Wednesday, September 9, 1953. The first official meeting of the contestants with the judges began, however, each morning at a breakfast conference held in the Hotel Shelbourne. At this meeting, the contestants would be judged on Intellect and Personality. Among the judges that year was movie star Jeannette MacDonald.[13] Having met the judges, the contestants were ready for the preliminary nights' programs.

The 1953 *Miss America Pageant* program was produced and directed by George Buzby, son of J. Howard Buzby who had resigned after thirteen years with the *Miss America Pageant*. George Buzby had been trained by his father since 1946 in all production aspects. George had designed the sets for the 1950 *Miss America Pageant*. In 1953 he was named co-producer with his father. He took over the entire production responsibilities after his father resigned.[14]

Another change in the *Miss America Pageant* personnel was in its Master of Ceremonies. The pageant Master of Ceremonies that year would be radio announcer Al Owen. Owen was given the job on the first night of preliminaries after the scheduled Master of Ceremonies, Marty May, left due to illness.[15]

Besides the change in Master of Ceremonies, there was still another last-minute change in the 1953 *Miss America Pageant's* cast. Although the evenings' programs were scheduled to begin with organ music played by Atlantic City organist Lois Miller, another organist, Doris Giacobbe, opened the show instead. Miller, who had been the pageant organist "for years," would not play in 1953 because of her husband's death.[16]

With the cast, the supporting personnel, and the contestants finally confirmed, the "show" was ready to begin. As in the past, with only slight content variations, the format for the three nights' "shows" was identical. For the 1953 preliminaries, the contestants would be divided into three competition groups. On Wednesday, the first group of seventeen would compete in the evening gown competition; the second group of eighteen in the swimsuit competition; the third group of seventeen in the talent competition. On Thursday, the second group would compete in evening gown, the third group in swimsuit, and the first group in talent. On the final night of preliminaries, the third group would compete in evening gown, the first group would compete in swimsuit, and the second group would compete in talent.[17]

The only other differences in the preliminary programs from night to night were in the content and cast of the entertainment between the swimsuit competitions and the talent competitions. On Wednesday night, the audience was entertained by singer Mel Tormé; on Thursday night by ventriloquist Paul Winchell and dummy Jerry Mahoney; on Friday night by variety performers Bambi Lynn and Rod Alexander.[18]

The program of preliminaries opened each night with organ music, followed by the Overture played by the Miss America Orchestra under the direction of Harold Ferrin. The overture complete, the show began with the presentation of the contestants in a number titled "The Gems of the Ocean." For this number, George Buzby created the illusion of an underwater scene. As the house lights dimmed, the stage lights behind the curtains revealed numerous water-fountain jets spraying into the air. Giant aquatic plants suspended in air over the stage area added to the underwater imagery.

As the water surging from the jets subsided, the fifty two contestants were revealed, each garbed in different color gowns. Al Owen introduced each one to the audience in alphabetical order beginning with Miss Alabama. After her introduction each walked down the runway. After each contestant had been introduced, the national anthem was played. Following the anthem, the judges were introduced to the audience. During the introductions, the next scene was being prepared.[19]

The next event on the program was the preliminary evening gown competition. For this segment of the program, Buzby continued his aquatic theme. As each contestant was introduced, an undersea diver appeared to lift her from a huge treasure chest. While each contestant promenaded down the runway, for the first time in *Miss America Pageant* history, male singers provided background music.[20]

After the evening gown competition came the swimsuit competition. For this segment, Buzby sprawled a giant net over the stage, and by way of introduction, the girls were "spilled" [like a giant catch-of-the-day] onto the platform. The contestants, in their swimsuits and high heeled shoes, paraded individually down the runway for the audience and the judges. As in the evening gown competition, songs provided by unidentified male singers accompanied the girls' stroll down the runway. After this competition, as stated previously, entertainment was provided by guest artists.[21]

The next event was the talent competition.[22] For the most part, the 1953 contestants sang, danced, or recited poetry. Two contestants offered a different fare. Miss West Virginia, Pat Seward, impersonated various popular singers. The other contestant, Miss Michigan, Velva Irene Robbins, a fourth-grade teacher, "taught" a lesson on the shortcomings of the American school system. After the last performer presented her talent, the audience was further entertained by a "Former Scholarship Winner."[23]

The evenings' programs ended with still another of Buzby's visual spectacles. For the final presentation, all fifty-two contestants appeared on stage holding clusters of lights. Miss America 1953, Neva Jane Langley was introduced to the audience. An "attendant" appeared with her also holding a cluster of lights. As Langley climbed the stairs to her throne, her long gown flowed over the staircase.[24]

The program was concluded each night with the announcement of the preliminary swimsuit and talent contest winners. They were:

Wednesday:
    Evelyn Ay, Miss Pennsylvania, Swimsuit
    Anne Lee Ceglis, Miss Virginia, Talent
Thursday:
    Elaine Lois Holkenbrink, Miss Wyoming, Swimsuit
    Delores Jerde, Miss South Dakota, Talent
Friday:
    Patricia Ann Johns, Miss California, Swimsuit
    Lois Ann Alava, Miss Delaware, Talent

Between 5,800 and 7,000 people attended the different nights of preliminary programs.[25]

*Finals*

The 1953 *Miss America Pageant* began at 8:30 p.m. on Saturday, September 12, 1953. Convention Hall, with a seating capacity of 25,000, was completely sold out.[26]

Basically, the program for the Finals was exactly the same as for the preliminary contests with a few variations. As in the preliminaries, the show began with organ music by Doris Giacobbe. The show continued with the overture, and the presentation of the contestants in the "Gems of the Ocean," number.[27]

This number was a bit different from those in previous nights. On Saturday night, the contestants were blocked on stage in staggered lines. Each hid her face with a fan. After accepting the audience's applause, the contestants turned to salute Miss America 1953, Neva Jane Langley, who appeared seated upon her throne. The throne was positioned atop a platform which rose from ground level to a vantage point overlooking the proceedings:

As the orchestra played a regal march, she gracefully stepped down the long stairway leading to the runway, smiling beautifully as the floodlights sparkled on her white gown and crown. She strode the runway as the orchestra played "A Pretty Girl is Like a Melody," and there appeared to be tears in her eyes as she made the turn at the end of the runway and headed back to the main stage . . . .[28]

After Miss America's processional march, the other contestants, including Miss Atlantic City, Jean Marie Brownrigg, took their stroll down the runway. After all were back on stage in their places, the national anthem was played. After the anthem, Al Owen announced the ten semi-finalists. They were:

    1. Miss Alabama, Virginia McDavid
    2. Miss California, Patricia Ann Johns
    3. Miss Delaware, Lois Ann Alava

4. Miss Mississippi, Susanne Dugger
5. Miss New York City, Joan Cecilia Kaible
6. Miss Oregon, Patti Elaine Throop
7. Miss Pennsylvania, Evelyn Ay
8. Miss South Carolina, Miriam Jacqueline Stevenson
9. Miss Virginia, Anne Lee Ceglis
10. Miss Wyoming, Elaine Holkenbrink[29]

The program continued with the introduction of the Judges. After this, the ten Semi-Finalists competed in Evening Gown. The competition was held in front of the same set as in the preliminaries, and followed the same procedure. All the semi-finalists were wearing white gowns.[30]

After the Evening Gown competition came the Swimsuit Competition, which was set in the same setting as in the preliminaries. Like the Evening Gown Competition, it too was staged in the same manner as in the preliminaries. Upon completion of the Swimsuit Competition, the twenty one remaining contestants were introduced to the audience. The program continued as follows:

a) Entertainment by an unidentified "former scholarship winner."
b) Ten Semi-finalists in the Talent Competition
c) Presentation of second half of the remaining non semi-finalist contestants.
d) Presentation of Most Talented Non-Finalist Award (Trophy and $1,000) to Miss South Dakota, Delores Jerde.
e) Presentation of Miss Congeniality Award ($1,000) to Miss New Jersey, Patricia Ann Condon.[31]

At this point activity ceased briefly for a "Panorama Interlude" while the Judges made their decision on who would be the top five finalists. Their names were announced after the interlude. They were: Miss Pennsylvania, Miss New York City, Miss Virginia, Miss Alabama, and Miss Mississippi. For the 1953 *Miss America Pageant*, as in all pageants since 1947, all of the finalists were asked the same two questions. Those questions were (paraphrased):[32]

1. What place in the world would the contestant select to continue her studies?
2. What were the qualities of a good citizen?

While the judges made their decision, another "former scholarship winner" performed for the audience. Next, the parade trophies, which had been announced previously, were presented on stage. Just prior to the announcement of Miss America 1954, Miss America 1953, Neva Jane Langley took her final walk down the runway. The announcement of the four runners-up and Miss America 1954 followed. The fourth runner-up was Miss Mississippi, Susanne Dugger; the third runner-up was Miss Alabama, Virginia McDavid; the second runner-up was Miss Virginia, Anne Lee Ceglis; the first runner-up was Miss New York City, Joan Cecilia Kaible; Miss America 1954, was Miss Pennsylvania, Evelyn Ay.[33]

Miss America's prizes included $5,000 in scholarships and a new car, and a guaranteed $40,000 in personal appearances throughout the year. Upon receiving her crown, scepter, and "royal robes," Ay, fighting back tears, exclaimed, "...it [is] impossible for me to express an emotion so deeply felt."[34]

Evelyn Ay recalls:

> It was such an emotional moment...Not only for me but for my family as well...My fiance Carl [who was not at the pageant] heard about my victory on the radio.
>
> [The pageant] was a wonderful experience for me as it is for every girl who enters...people don't realize what the program does for a girl in Oshkosh.[35]

The *Miss America Pageant* of 1953, would be the last one to be restricted by space to Atlantic City. Next year, the pageant would be beamed across the United States. With this, the girl next door would parade in her swimsuit right into your very bedroom if that's where your television was. To paraphrase Morse, what would this change wrought?

# Chapter VI
# 1954: (Almost) Live from Atlantic City

After approximately thirty-three years of on-and-off existence, the *Miss America Pageant* added a new dimension to its presentation—television coverage. The question of how the advent of television would change the pageant was not exclusively a concern of media theorists. This same question was contemplated by the *Miss America Pageant* organizers for quite some time. Although a media researcher might look at television's effect on the event's structure, the pageant organizers' worries were purely fiscal. The argument on how the pageant's televising would affect the gate receipts at Convention Hall was of utmost concern.[1]

It was this very question that precluded the televising of the pageant in 1953. That year, the American Broadcasting Company (ABC) had placed a bid with the *Miss America Pageant* organizers for the exclusive rights to televise the National Finals. The *Miss America Pageant* Board would not even consider accepting this offer unless ABC agreed that Philadelphia and other neighboring communities would be "blacked-out" from any television coverage. This stipulation was based on several factors. That year the ticket cost had doubled in price from the previous year. Fearing that this price increase combined with the "free" home viewing would hurt the pageant financially, the *Miss America Pageant* Board of Directors, perhaps not foreseeing the lucrative potential in broadcasting the event, declined ABC's offer. The telecasting of the *Miss America Pageant* in 1953 was not to be.[2]

In July of 1954, *Miss America Pageant* President Hugh Wathen once again met with ABC Vice President Paul Whiteman to discuss the possibility of a 1954 telecast. A tentative agreement was reached, pending *Miss America Pageant* Board approval. The Board was concerned that gate receipts would fall.[3]

The Board's pecuniary apprehensions were allayed somewhat by the $10,000 fee which would be paid to the *Miss America Pageant* for ABC's exclusive telecast rights. An additional $12,500 for endorsement rights were paid by corporate sponsors.[4]

Within one week of the ABC/*Miss America Pageant* meeting, the Philco Corporation contracted with the *Miss America Pageant* to sponsor the telecast. By so doing, Philco became the fourth sponsor for the 1954 *Miss America Pageant* telecast. The other three sponsors were Joseph Bancroft and Sons, Nash Motors, and the Florida Citrus commission. Between one hundred twenty-five and one hundred thirty ABC stations would carry the pageant with additional stations "hooking-up" at 11:00 p.m. After playing solely to Atlantic City audiences for thirty three years, the *Miss America Pageant* Finals would finally be seen from coast to coast on Saturday, September 11, 1954—though only for the last ninety minutes.[5]

Although the Saturday finals would begin at 8:30 p.m., television coverage would commence at 10:30 p.m.[5] At that time, the five television cameras would pick up the live action as it happened. Included in those ninety minutes were a) the talent competition, b) the selection of the five finalists, c) the speeches of the five finalists in response to questions, the naming of the runners-up, and the crowning of Miss America.[6]

Still apprehensive that somehow the television coverage would force changes on the traditional pageant format, *Miss America Pageant* officials insisted that coverage should be non-intrusive. ABC cameras would be allowed to cover the pageant as a news event only, presenting the action "as-is" without any directorial input or intervention. Although introduced to the live audience, the commentary offered by anchor persons Bess Myerson and John Daly from a backstage studio would be heard by the home viewers only.[7]

To further insure that television coverage would not interfere with the Convention Hall audience, ABC agreed to position its five cameras in such a way as not to block the audience's view.[8]

With all the arrangements finalized, the "marriage" of the *Miss America Pageant* and television would finally be "consummated." The 1954 competitions were ready to begin.

### The 1954 Miss America Pageant: Day One

The 1954 pageant was different from its predecessors in more than one way. Besides being the first pageant to be televised, the 1954 *Miss America Pageant*, unlike other *Miss America Pageants*, held its traditional parade at night. The parade, heralded as a history-making, illuminated night parade, was scheduled to begin at 8:30 p.m. on Tuesday, September 7, 1954.[9]

According to reports, "[A night parade would] be cooler for both spectators and marchers. It [would] also give more people a chance to view the many floats, bands and girls."[10]

After solving various logistical problems, the idea for the Illuminated Night Parade was proposed to the mayor of every community in Southern New Jersey by Hugh L. Wathen, President of the *Miss America Pageant*.[11] The idea was well received, with all the mayors attending the dinner-meeting agreeing to enter a representative float in the parade.

At approximately 8:30 p.m., a burst of four "cannon crackers" announced the commencement of the parade. Over one hundred and twelve units took part in the two and one half hour, two mile parade. Included in the line of march down the Boardwalk were nine marching bands, fifteen colorful Philadelphia Mummers String Bands, and thirty-four floats. Each float was provided with a generator by the *Miss America Pageant* organization for illumination purposes. The 1954 floats were considered by some to be among the most elaborate floats in years.[12]

Heading the parade line-up was Miss America 1946, Marilyn Buferd, acting as Grand Marshal. After her came the American Legion Band of Salem (New Jersey) and the Marine Corps Color Guard.[13] The main attraction followed—the fifty contestants vying for the title of Miss America 1955.

Leading the procession of beauties was the float bearing Miss America 1954, Evelyn Ay. After this float, the contestants rolled down the Boardwalk in automobiles provided by Nash Motors, one of the pageant's sponsors. The contestants' cars appeared in the parade line in alphabetical order according to state name. Each contestant wore furs provided by two Atlantic City furriers, Koff Furs and Polansky-Lane-Shuman. One contestant, Miss North Carolina, Betty Jo Ring, had as an escort the seventy-five piece Lexington High School Band. To make the trek to Atlantic City, the Lexington High students had raised $2,700 by selling school rings. Miss North Carolina was an English teacher at Lexington High.[14]

Over two hundred thousand people lined the Boardwalk to catch a glimpse of the parade. According to reports:

The 1954 Illuminated Night Parade was witnessed by an all-time record breaking audience and acknowledged to be the greatest outdoor spectacle ever staged in the resort.[15]

For all the acclaimed success, the first Illuminated Night Parade made pageant history in another unexpected way. According to reports, just at about the time the first float passed the reviewing stand at Convention Hall, "the clouds opened, and a blanket of rain fell."[16] This was the first time that rain had dampened the pageant parade's festive atmosphere. Astonishingly enough, both the crowds and the parade participants remained. It is reported that one onlooker commented, "If [the contestants] can take it, so can we...[a]t least we're more dressed than they are."[17]

First, second and third place awards were given to floats in the municipal, hotel, commercial and state divisions.[18]

*Preliminaries*

The first official meeting of the contestants with the judges took place on Wednesday morning, September 8, 1954 at 9:00 a.m. at a breakfast held in Haddon Hall. The judges for the 1954 *Miss America Pageant* were: Dr. Paul Anderson, president of the Pennsylvania College for Women; Dr. Paul D. Bagwell, head of the Communications Skills Department, Michigan State College; Mini Benzell, opera and concert performer; LaMar Buckner, President of Utah's Junior Chamber of Commerce; Grace Kelly, motion picture star; Venus Ramey, Miss America, 1944; Deems Taylor, music critic; Paul Whiteman, music educator; and Coby Whitmore, magazine artist and illustrator.[19]

Having met the judges, the contestants were ready to begin production rehearsals for the preliminary nights' programs. From Wednesday, September 8 through Friday, September 10, 1954, preliminary eliminations would be held at Convention Hall in front of the judges and the live audience. That year's *Miss America Pageant* program would be produced by Broadway producer Vinton Freedley, instead of George Buzby who had asked for a leave of absence.[20]

With only slight content variations, the format for the three nights' "shows" was identical. Although the interim entertainment provided between competition events varied only slightly from night to night, the main difference in the program was in the competition itself.[21]

For the preliminaries, the fifty contestants would be divided into three competition groups. On Wednesday, the first group would compete in the evening gown competition, the second group in the swimsuit competition, and the third group in the talent competition. On Thursday, the second group would compete in evening gown, the third group in swimsuit, and the first group in talent. On the final night of preliminaries, the third group would compete in evening gown, the first group would compete in swimsuit, and the second group would compete in talent.[22]

The afternoon rehearsals conducted by Master of Ceremonies, Bob Russell, lasted approximately three hours. During these rehearsals, Russell would

[give] each girl pointers on how to make her entrance, showing them each little gesture, introducing soft music here and increasing tempo there—all that they would be at their best before the footlights.[23]

The evenings' program began each night at 8:30 p.m. with an organ prelude played on the console Convention Hall's organ by Atlantic City organist, Lois Miller. The orchestra, under the direction of Max Meth, picked up the last strains of Miller's prelude, and according to reports, "the...preliminary contest[s] [were] under way."[24]

While the orchestra played their musical "Salute to George Gershwin," "the house lights faded, and the production...began to unfold under the battery of gleaming spots." The lights on stage revealed the fifty contestants grouped around a wishing well. To begin the affair, host Bob Russell appeared on stage and sang his original composition, "By the Wishing Well."[25]

While Russell sang, each of the contestants holding American Beauty Roses took an introductory bow from the stage. Commencing with Miss Alabama, the traditional "Parade of States" proceeded, from the stage to the newly erected "Y-shaped" runway which jutted out towards the center of Convention Hall. The contestants formed two columns down the runway. As the Orchestra and Russell sang "This is Miss America," Miss America 1954, Evelyn Ay, walked down the runway between the two columns of contestants. After reaching the end of the runway, the National Anthem was played. To conclude the "Boardwalk Promenade," there was a reprise of "This is Miss America," as Ay and all the contestants returned to the stage and then walked off to prepare for the upcoming competitions. After this, Miss Atlantic City, Marilyn Ross, acting as a non-competitive hostess, greeted the audience.[26]

According to reports, "flashbulbs glittered like a myriad of lightning bugs in the darkened reaches of the auditorium" at the beginning of the evening gown competition. The Wishing Well set for the opening "Boardwalk Promenade" was replaced by a large marine shell setting. It was from this marine shell setting that each individual contestant emerged as her name and state were announced. From the seashell, the contestants walked down the runway. Although there would be no announced winner for evening gown, points were still given which counted towards the selection of the top ten finalists.[27]

Between the evening gown competition and the next event, the swim suit competition, there was some divertissement. On Wednesday, this divertissement came from a group called the Acromaniacs; on Thursday from The Murphy Sisters; on Friday from the Gaudsmith Brothers.[28]

After the divertissement, the swimsuit competition began. Like the evening gown competition, the contestants walked down the runway. All wore one piece bathing suits and high heeled shoes. The winner for each night of swimsuit competition would be announced at the program's end.[29]

Before the next and last competition event, another divertissement was slotted. On Wednesday that divertissement was offered by Anne Lee Ceglis, Miss Virginia, 1953; on Thursday, Joan Kaible, Miss New York City, 1953; on Friday, Anne Lee Ceglis performed again.[30]

The final competition event was the talent competition. During this hour-long segment, the contestants were judged on their talent presentations. In the 1954 *Miss America Pageant* preliminaries, the range of talent included opera and pop singing, dramatic monologues, instrumental interpretations, dancing, interior decorating, and ventriloquism. The winner of the talent competition would be announced at the end of each program.[31]

Before the audience could hear the outcome of each night's preliminary competition, they first would hear words of greeting from a "special guest." This special guest was Makaoyatodutawin, Miss Indian America II, a.k.a., Mary Louise DeFonder. Makaoyatodutawin, which means "Woman of the Red Earth People" in Yanktonais Sioux, "extended greetings to the audience in behalf of her people."

The program was concluded each night with the announcement of the preliminary swimsuit and talent contest winners. They were:

Wednesday:
> Lee Ann Meriwether, Miss California, Swimsuit
> Linda Maude Weisbrod, Miss District of Colombia, Talent

Thursday:
> Gloria Daniel, Miss Florida, Swimsuit

Janice Hutton Somers, Miss Michigan, Talent (tie)
Heather Jo Taferner, Miss New York City, Talent (tie)
Friday:
Polly Rankin Suber, Miss South Carolina, Swimsuit
Barbara Maxine Quinlan, Miss Ohio, Talent

Approximately 6,000 people attended Wednesday's preliminary; approximately 7,000 attended on Thursday; approximately 6,100 attended on Friday.[32]

### Finals

Over 18,000 people attended the 1954 *Miss America Pageant* at Convention Hall. More than two hours before the beginning of the 1954 *Miss America Pageant* Finals several thousand people had already lined up outside of Convention Hall "as they waited for the doors to open and make their way to choice balcony seats."[33] The audience seated, at 8:30 p.m. it was "on with the show."

Basically, the program for the Finals was exactly the same as for the preliminary contests with a few variations. As in the preliminaries, the show began with organ music by Lois Miller. The show continued with the overture, the "Boardwalk Promenade," the "Wishing Well," "The Parade of States," the introduction of Miss America 1954, and the National Anthem. This was followed by the welcome from Miss Atlantic City and the presentation of the judges. At this point the show diverged from its preliminaries format.[34]

Now the ten semi-finalists were announced to the audience. They were:

1. Miss Alabama, Marilyn Jean Tate
2. Miss California, Lee Meriwether
3. Miss Chicago, Regina Janine Dombeck
4. Miss District of Colombia, Linda Maude Weisbrod
5. Miss Florida, Ann Gloria Daniels
6. Miss Michigan, Janice Hutton
7. Miss Ohio, Barbara Maxine Quinlan
8. Miss Pennsylvania, Barbara Sue Nager
9. Miss South Carolina, Polly Rankin Suber
10. Miss Tennessee, Gerry Johnson

The program continued as follows:

1. Evening Gown Competition
2. Panorama Interlude
3. Divertissement: Ann Lee Ceglis, Miss Virginia, 1953
4. Miss Indian America II
5. Swim Suit Competition
6. Presentation of Boardwalk Parade Awards
7. Divertissement: Joan Kaible, Miss New York City, 1953
8. Divertissement: Delores Jerde, Miss South Dakota, 1953
9. Presentation of Miss Congeniality Award ($1,000) to Miss Illinois, Patsy (Pat) Bruce

10. Presentation of Special Non-talent Award (Non-Finalist)
11. Talent Competition[35]

At 10:25 p.m. the television lights were turned on stage. At 10:30 p.m. the first *Miss America Pageant* was broadcast. According to Lee Meriwether, the telecast picked up the action during the last three talent competitions. After the competition Bob Russell announced the winner of the Talent Trophy and the names of the Five Finalists. They were: Miss California, Miss Florida, Miss South Carolina, Miss Pennsylvania, and Miss Michigan.[36]

At this point, all of the contestants but one were taken off stage. According to Lee Meriwether, "The five finalists were asked the same three questions, with the girls off-stage unable to hear each other's answers." Those questions were:[37]

1. How would [you] use your scholarship fund?
2. What would be [your] most vivid memory of the Atlantic City Pageant?
3. What [do you think] of the responsibilities of Miss America?

After all five finalists had answered the questions, they were escorted off stage where a backstage camera took up the action. The winners starting with fourth runner-up were announced from back stage to the television audience. The fourth runner-up was Miss Michigan, Janice Hutton; the third runner up was Miss Pennsylvania, Barbara Sue Nager; the second runner-up was Miss South Carolina, Polly Sue Rankin.[38] Lee Meriwether recalls the final moments, "Ann Daniels, Miss Florida...was first runner-up. I had picked her to win." Lee Meriwether was the new Miss America—the first to be crowned on television. In her words:

I was crying hysterically. I had lost my father in June and had said, 'I hope Daddy knows, and I hope he's proud.' I think that's the correct quote. Other people remember it differently, and as they have lost the kinescope of the telecast, there is no record.

I remember Bess [Myerson] interviewing my mother and me backstage next to a Philco set...I was still crying and my mother brought me out of it beautifully with a typical mother's response, 'Stop your sniffling.' Bess asked her to repeat it and Mommie nearly died. She had not realized we were on t.v.[39]

Miss America 1954, Evelyn Ay, placed the crown on her successor's head without so much as a word. Earlier during her presentation, Miss Ay had said the following brief words:

I am writing the last chapter in my long golden book of memories. It is bound in the love and friendliness of the American people, and I will read and re-read this book, the Life of Miss America 1953, her year of happiness.[40]

This was the last time that Evelyn Ay as Miss America would speak. Though known for her oratorical talent, she was told that since the crowning was being telecast, she would not be able to say Miss America's traditional farewell.[41]

As Bob Russell sang "The Spirit of Miss America" Miss America 1955 was presented to a cheering though annoyed crowd. According to Meriwether:

The Atlantic City Audience was so upset that the TV audience saw me get the news backstage, that the following year, Miss America was announced and informed on stage.[42]

Miss America's prizes included $5,000 in scholarships, a mink stole, an ermine stole, jewelry, a screen test with Warner Brothers, and an appearance on *What's My Line*. In addition, she was given an opportunity of a lifetime. In her words:

as Philco was a sponsor, I was given the opportunity to appear on *The Philco Television Playhouse* twice, in starring roles. The real beginning of my career—I've always been so very lucky!

The 1954 *Miss America Pageant* was watched by 27 million viewers in 8,714,000 homes. It received a 20.9 rating, and a 39 share of the audience.[43]

### Changes Between 1955 and 1963

The following are some of the more noticeable changes in the *Miss America Pageant* between 1955 and 1963. The changes:

1955    Bert Parks took over as host.
        Glen Osser, Staff Conductor at NBC, was named musical director.

1956    Television co-anchor with former Miss America was newsman Peter Donald.

1957    Non-finalist talent awards in different categories were established.
        $30,000 was budgeted to design and purchase better lighting equipment after observing the 1956 kinescope.
        The *Miss America Pageant* was telecast by CBS.
        'The outmoded official Miss America robe was redesigned....'
        The television co-anchor with former Miss America was newsman Douglas Edwards.

1958    The telecast increased to two hours.
        The contestants were introduced to the audience minus the semi-finalists. The semi-finalists were then introduced to the television audience.

1959    A half-hour telecast of the parade was presented on CBS.
        By 1959 every state was represented.

The first Miss America: Margaret Gorman, Miss America 1921. Photo credit:
The Press of Atlantic City.

Miss America 1922-23, Mary Campbell. Notice the policeman in beach attire.
Photo credit: The Press of Atlantic City.

Evelyn Ay, the last Miss America before television, crowns the first television queen, Lee Meriwether, Miss America 1955. Photo credit: The Press of Atlantic City.

Vonda VanDyke, Miss America 1965. Photo credit: Color by Currier.

Former Miss Americas reunited at the 50th anniversary of the pageant. Photo credit: Color by Currier.

Rebecca King crowns Shirley Cothran at the 1974 pageant. Photo credit: Color by Currier.

Miss New Jersey 1980, interviewed by a former Miss New Jersey turned reporter, in front of the map of the

Ron Ely, 1980 host, and Bert Park's replacement. Photo courtesy of Therese Hanley.

Ron gets a message never seen by home audiences. Photo courtesy of Therese Hanley.

Miss America 1981 and her court. Note the police officer providing security. First from left is Lencola Sullivan, first black to make top five. Sullivan would later be implicated by the tabloids in the Bill Clinton presidential campaign extra-marital affair scandal. Photo courtesy of Therese Hanley, 4th from left.

Former Miss Americas reunited in 1983. Photo credit: Color by Currier

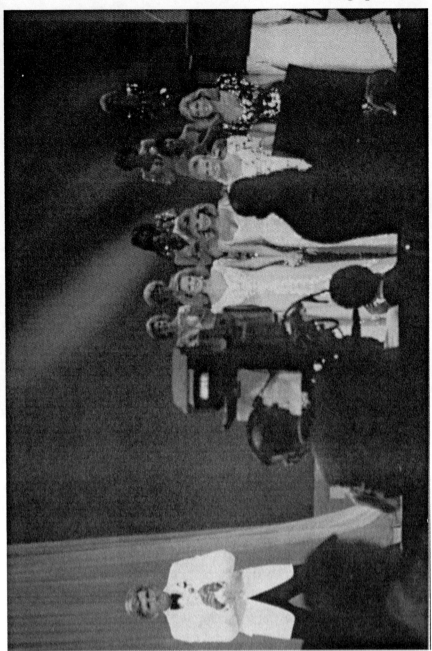

Gary Collins awaits the judges' decision during the 1984 telecast. The judges took longer than usual. Collins asks, "What would Bert do?" Photo credit: Color by Currier.

Suzette Charles crowns Sharlene Wells during the 1984 pageant. Photo credit:
Color by Currier.

Miss America meets the press immediately after the show's conclusion. Photo credit: Color by Currier.

Miss America and founding father Adrian Phillips. Photo courtesy: Color by Currier.

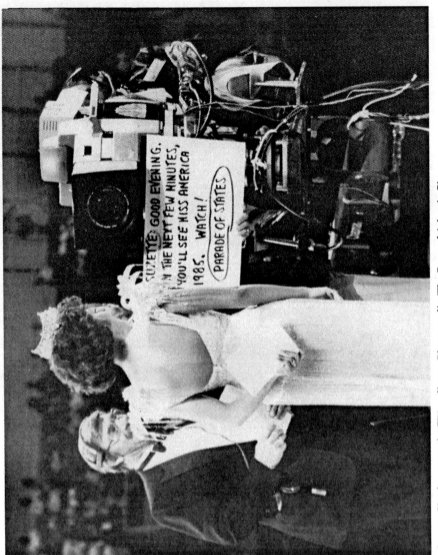

Suzette Charles greets the TV audience. Photo credit: The Press of Atlantic City.

Leonard Horn (L) and Al Marks (R) hold press conference after the "Vanessa Incident." Photo credit: The Press of Atlantic City.

Gary Collins and Bert Parks at the 1990 pageant. Gary left the show the following year. Bert died in 1992. Photo credit: The Press of Atlantic City.

The Boardwalk Parade. Photo credit: The Press of Atlantic City.

Boardwalk reveller "showing his shoes." Photo credit: The Press of Atlantic City.

Informal parade tradition "Show us your shoes." Photo credit: Color by Currier.

Convention Hall. Photo credit: Colorado Camicia.

Leonora Slaughter and Bess Myerson. Photo credit: Color by Currier.

# Chapter VII
# The Status Quo Sixties

The sixties, long known for being the psychedelic, peace, love, happiness, war-torn, revolutionary, bra-burning, draft-dodging, protesting, civil-rights, liberating sixties existed everywhere in the United States, it seems, but in Miss America land. It would not be until the late sixties that dissent, demonstrations, controversy and commotion would come to Convention Hall. For the most part, the sixties were the status quo sixties at least as far as the pageant was concerned. The world might be teetering on the eve of destruction, but all was right in Atlantic City, which to home viewers might well have been another era or Oz.

While the world of Miss America seemed not to change as far as values, philosophy, and image, hidden ferment was taking place, however. That catalyst of change was television which even in its honeymoon stage with the pageant was already pounding away at the pageant's structure. As will be demonstrated in future chapters, television was making its mark though so gradually and subtly that even the most liberal of Miss America fans could rest assured that all was safe, familiar, and well on the home front.

### The Early Sixties

Nineteen sixty marked the pageant's 40th anniversary. As such, the theme of the pageant was the "Royal Reunion."[1] An important addition to the festivities was the hiring of an outside choreographer, Lola Coates. From that year and thereafter, choreography and dance would be part of the Miss America Pageant—an addition that would become more intricate and integral to the form and flow of the televised presentation. The choreography during the early sixties was simple in its complexity and sterile in its sensuality. Rather than being interwoven as part of the flow of the action, choreography for the most part consisted of self-contained entre-acts demarcating the beginning and end of competition events. As will be seen in later chapters, as the years progressed dance became more and more a part of the Pageant's "look." Its importance as a vehicle with which to move the action from scene to scene as well as a means of spicing the pace and visual variety was quickly noted. As the years progressed, the dances became, if not more torrid, at least more contemporary. It is ironic that while the stagers of the pageant leave no stone unturned in creating a pristine Miss America environment, the erotically clad Miss America dancers bump and grind with a ferocity incongruent with the rest of the setting. That, however, would be in the future. In the early sixties, choreography was still in keeping with the sanctity of Miss Americadom. In 1960, the first year where outside choreography was recruited, the cast included eight former Miss Americas and two male dancers. Men had invaded the hallowed Hall. The cast from the sixties until the present would also include popular professional entertainers. This cast addition as well as the use of male dancers has not sat well with some former Miss Americas who believe that the shows have become to the pageant what gambling has become to Las Vegas or Atlantic City. Some Miss Americas feel that the pageant entertainment should include the non-finalist talent award winners.[2]

Other important changes occurred in the telecast in the early sixties. In 1961, for example, the pageant increased its coverage to two and one half hours. In 1963, the telecast's duration was cut to two hours.[3] Part of the change in duration time had to do with the change from non-intrusive news format to variety show/contest. As such, the newsman anchor position was abolished. Former Miss Americas would thereafter act as television anchors.[4]

Nineteen sixty one would also be the last year for the telecasting of the Boardwalk Parade by any major network.[5] The show was the thing, and therefore, the colorful but very local parade was of no interest to television.

Further changing the character of the pageant and defining its identity as a national Pageant packaged for a coast to coast audience was the exclusion of any participation by contestants not holding a state title. Among those titles to "bite the dust" in the early sixties were Miss Atlantic City, Miss Puerto Rico (1962), Miss Chicago, Miss Canada, and Miss New York City (1963). Only states would be represented in 1964.[6] The *Miss America Pageant* was no longer a local occurrence. Television had erased Atlantic City's boundaries and proclaimed, "Here is your Miss, America." The pageant was now the Big Time—cities and commonwealths need not apply.

Perhaps the most important change or at least an important catalyst of change was the introduction of a new television producer, John Koushouris, who has been with the pageant from 1962 until the present.[7]

### The 1964 Miss America Pageant

*Boardwalk Parade*

The 1964 *Miss America Pageant* officially began at 8:30 p.m. on Tuesday, September 8, 1964, with the traditional, illuminated Boardwalk Parade. Tickets for seats along the parade route down the Boardwalk were available at $5 for Grandstand and $1.50 for Bleachers.[8]

Over 150,000 spectators attended the parade which included, "lovely ladies, [forty] lavish floats, and lilting marching units." The parade lasted for ninety minutes, a cut in time from previous years when there had been long delays in the passing of different units.[9]

As in the past, the parade line-up was headed by the Grand Marshal. This year it was Perle Mesta. She was followed by the float carrying Miss America 1964, Donna Axum, bands, commercial and civic floats, and of course, those carrying the fifty contestants vying for the 1965 Miss America crown.[10]

With variations in content and "the cast of players," for the most part, the 1964 Parade was pretty much like the 1954 parade with one major exception—Miss Atlantic City, the traditional non-competing "hostess" who had been a part of the festivities since the first pageant. In previous years, Miss Atlantic City's float was among the first in the parade line-up. This was not the case in 1964. Although pageant sources state that the title of Miss Atlantic City was discontinued in 1960, according to reports there was a Miss Atlantic City in the 1964 pageant parade.

Curiously though, after the 1964 parade there would be no Miss Atlantic City in the same capacity ever again. Patricia M. Manno, who held that position that year, resigned abruptly after the parade.[11]

Manno contended that she had been the victim of a political backlash against her uncle, Democrat Labor Consultant Peter Manno, who had had recent disputes with New Jersey Republican State Senator Frank Farley. Miss Manno claimed that she had been snubbed by *Miss America Pageant* organizers for this reason. Adding to the "snub" was her float's placement in the parade line-up—thirty-first out of forty.[12] Other than this, the parade progressed without incident.

Winners in various divisions were named in the Atlantic City Press the following day. First, second, and third place awards were given to floats in the hotel, banks and utilities, restaurant and candy shops, boating and fishing themes, commercial, visiting state, visiting communities, chamber of commerce, and civic clubs divisions.[13]

### Preliminaries

As in the past, ten finalists would be selected during three nights of competition. This selection would be based upon points accumulated in the swimsuit, evening gown, and talent competitions held on Wednesday, Thursday, and Friday nights of Pageant week. In addition to these public competitions, private interviews with the judges would be held during the afternoon.[14]

The judges for the 1964 *Miss America Pageant* were:

1. June Allyson, movie star
2. James T. Aubrey, Jr., President of Columbia Broadcasting System
3. John Brownlee, Director of the Manhattan School of Music
4. Elizabeth Dyer, chair[person] of the National Panhellenic Conference
5. Richard H. Headlee, immediate past-President of the U.S. Junior Chamber of Commerce
6. John K. M. McCaffrey, television personality
7. Nettie Rosenstien, fashion designer
8. Ted Thorpe, President of Cinegraf Productions, Inc.
9. Marilyn Van Derbur, Miss America, 1958
10. J. Leonard Reinsch, President of Cox Broadcasting Corporation.[15]

The judging system for the 1964 *Miss America Pageant* allowed each judge to give five points to his or her choice for first place, four for second place, three for third, two for fourth and one for fifth in all competitions except talent. In the talent portion, points were worth double, *i.e.*, ten for first, and so on.[16] The ten contestants with the most accumulated points would move on to the finals on Saturday, September 12, 1964.

The 1964 *Miss America Pageant* program would be produced by Alexander Cantwell, and hosted by Bert Parks. As in the past, with only slight content variations, the format for the three nights' "shows" was identical. Although the interim "divertissement" between competition events varied only slightly from night to night, the main difference in the program was in the competition itself.[17]

For the preliminaries, the fifty state representatives were divided into three competition groups. On Wednesday, the "Red Group" would compete in the evening gown competition, the "Blue Group" in the swimsuit competition, and the "Gold Group" in the talent competition. On Thursday, the Blue Group would compete in evening gown, the Gold Group in swimsuit, and the Red Group in talent. On the final night of preliminaries, the Gold Group would compete in evening gown, the Red Group would compete in swimsuit, and the Blue Group would compete in talent.[18]

The evenings' programs began each night at 8:30 p.m. with the overture which was played by the Miss America Orchestra, under the direction of Glen Osser. The curtain opened, to reveal a large map of New Jersey. The voice of Master of Ceremonies, Bert Parks could be heard singing:

Things are looking great in the Garden State this year.

There's a special reason for a happy season this year.

For this year is a big year as we celebrate a happy date.

It's the three hundredth birthday of Miss America's home state.[19]

In the middle of this musical introduction, the lights behind the *Miss America Pageant* slowly came up, revealing a giant birthday cake with three hundred lit candles.[20] Upon completing the above musical introduction, the New Jersey *Miss America Pageant* was off with flying colors. Bert Parks entered stage left and continued singing the theme song, "Come to the Party." Joining him were the Lee Sullivan Singers and Miss America 1964's Court of Honor, Roseanne Tueller, Miss DC, 1963, Melissa Hetzel, Miss Vermont, 1963, Karen Raye Schwartz, Miss Kansas 1963, and Donna Marie Black, Miss Nebraska 1963. As the song progressed, all fifty contestants entered carrying large gift-wrapped boxes on which appeared the contestant's state title. The contestants filled all areas of the stage until the song ended.[21]

At this point Bert Parks explained the theme of the pageant to the audience. Having done this, Parks proceeded to introduce each contestant to the audience by state name. As Parks called the contestant's state name, the corresponding contestant walked center stage, stopped momentarily acknowledging the audience's applause. After this, each proceeded down the runway and back to the stage. All fifty contestants followed this procedure. To close the scene, all the contestants went to the birthday cake and "blew out" the candles. The program of events continued with the introduction of judges and some interim divertissement. The rest of the show was divided into three parts: "The Early Days," "Not So Long Ago," and "Up To Date."[22] These segments attempted to give some cohesion to the show based on the show's tercentenary theme. The segments, in actuality, served as musical vehicles for the different areas of competition.

The first segment, "The Early Days," served as the musical backdrop for the first phase of competition, the evening gown competition. This segment was set in a "colonial mansion" setting. This production number served as a prelude to the actual competition. As Bert Parks sang the title song, "Out of Yesterday," the contestants in the evening gown portion of the competition promenaded around the stage at the arm of escorts dressed in colonial costume. Upon completion of the number, Miss America 1964, Donna Axum, was introduced to the audience. Leaving her throne placed center stage, she strolled down the runway as the orchestra played "Miss America Song" ("There She Is"). Wearing her tiara and robe, Axum rounded the runway followed by the beam from a spot light and the applause of the audience.[23] The evening gown competition followed.

For this competition, each contestant was introduced by name, school affiliation, and state. The orchestra played incidental music as the "colonial escort" brought each contestant downstage. Upon introduction, that contestant walked center stage, turned to show her back, continued her turn, and then proceeded down the runway.[24]

The next segment, "Not So Long Ago," served as a prelude to the talent competition. This segment began with Parks' brief introduction of Roseanne Tueller, Miss Washington D. C., 1963, and Melissa Hetzel, Miss Vermont, 1963. After a few moments of jokes and banter, Tueller, Hetzel and Parks sang "The Old Soft Shoe" in front of the curtain. Straw hats and canes were used as props during this number. The talent competition followed, which was followed by some interim divertissement.[25]

The third segment, "Up To Date," featured a song called "Atlantic City." The setting for this musical number was a bi-level Atlantic City skyline, boardwalk rails and all. The number began with Parks singing the introduction to the title song. The curtains opened to reveal the set bustling with the hubbub of "extras." Miss America 1964 emerged from this rank and file, and picked up the song where Parks left off. The song claimed that Atlantic City was her second home. With this musical number as a warm-up, and the Atlantic City skyline as a backdrop, the swimsuit competition was next in the program. For this competition, the contestants were introduced by Parks by name and state affiliation. The procedure for the swimsuit competition was the same as for the evening gown competition. This competition was followed by interim divertissement.[26]

The show's finale was a production number titled "1/3 as Old as Methuselah." This number, sung in front of the curtain, featured Parks, the Court of Honor, and The Lee Sullivan Singers. Microphones on stands were propped up on the apron.[27]

The program concluded each night with the announcement of the preliminary swimsuit and talent contest winners. They were:

Wednesday:
   Sheri Lee Raap, Miss California, Swimsuit
   Barbara Hasselberg, Miss Minnesota, Talent
Thursday:
   Ella Dee Kessler, Miss West Virginia, Swimsuit
   Karen Kopseng, Miss North Dakota, Talent
Friday:
   Jane Nelson, Miss New Mexico, Swimsuit
   Vicki Powers, Miss Alabama, Talent

Approximately 5,826 people attended Wednesday's preliminary; approximately 6,198 attended on Thursday; approximately 7,148 attended on Friday.[28]

*Finals*

According to the Atlantic City Press, 17,647 people attended the 1964 *Miss America Pageant* Finals at Convention Hall. This audience—the live audience—in actuality experienced two shows. The "first show" began at 8:30 p.m. and lasted until 10:00 p.m. when the nationwide telecast was broadcast to 232 CBS television stations throughout the country. This "second show" was seen both by the Convention Hall Audience and by over 80 million home viewers in its two hour run.[29]

What were the differences between the "two shows" held that night, *i.e.*, the non-televised portion and the televised portion? Frank Deford explains the format for the finals (prior to 1971):

...for many years it was customary for the show in Convention Hall to start around 8:45. The ten semi-finalists would be revealed and the judging would actually begin. Then, at 10 o'clock the show would start all over again, the live audience would patiently go in the tank, and the ten winners would properly gasp and cry when they were announced.... The system was changed after [the first edition of this book] was published [in 1971]— detailing this charade—now [in 1978] the top ten is revealed for the first time before the camera.[30]

In 1964, the "reform" as described above by Deford had yet to occur. Before the cameras picked up the action at ten o'clock, the 1964 Pageant had, in actuality, already gotten underway.

According to the pageant program, the 1964 *Miss America Pageant* finals began at 8:30 p.m. with the overture. From here the program followed the preliminary night pageant's format with a few exceptions: a) "Come to the Party," b) Announcement of the ten semi-finalists, c) Presentation of the Judges, d) divertissement, e) "Out of Yesterday," f) Presentation of Miss

America, 1964, g) evening gown competition, h) "Atlantic City," i) swimsuit competition.[31] At this point, according to the pageant program, "At 10 P.M. the nationwide telecast begins over CBS-TV." As Deford reports, the program began all over again with everyone, including the live audience, joining in on the charade.

This portion of the program began with spotlights combing the audience at Convention Hall. Some of this audience had already taken their seats, others were caught walking to their seats. Next a drum roll was heard, overpowering the droll hum of people talking in the audience. A booming voice announced:

Live, from Convention Hall in Atlantic City, the 1964 Miss America Pageant (Fanfare). Your Master of Ceremonies, Bert Parks (Modulating Fanfare and applause). The Lee Sullivan Singers (Fanfare). Bess Myerson, one of the loveliest and most talented Miss Americas (fanfare). And starring from college and university campuses in every state of the union, the fifty lovely and talented girls competing for the title of Miss America.[32]

At this point the overture began. No action or narration took place immediately after, at least not for the live audience. For the following one minute and fifty seconds, the home audience saw sponsors' logos super-imposed on the screen with a voice over:

*Voice Over*
The 1964 *Miss America Pageant*—brought to you by Toni, creator of beauty products for the woman who prefers the natural look of beauty care at home. Oldsmobile, the rocket action car in behalf of your Olds dealer where the action is. And by Pepsi Cola, the official drink of the Pepsi Generation (dissolve to Bess Myerson, backstage, in actuality, with front stage action keyed in behind her).

*Bess Myerson*
Good evening and welcome to the night we've all been waiting for—the final and decisive night of the 1964 *Miss America Pageant*. This year the theme of the pageant celebrates the tercentenary, the three hundredth birthday of the State of New Jersey. The tradition of Miss America is not quite that old, however. The first pageant was held in Atlantic City in 1921. Since that time, there have been many imitations, but the Miss America Pageant has remained in a class by itself. Unchallenged for excitement, glamour, and ever increasing audience interest. Through the years, audience reaction to the pageant has been one of venerable pride in the bright image of our country's young women and tonight that pride will be justified once again when you at home and the audience here in Convention Hall meet the intelligent, attractive, talented young ladies who are the contenders for the title of Miss America 1965. During the past week, the girls have been experiencing the same emotions, anticipations, hopes, and doubts that have been felt by all Miss America contestants including myself. But these emotions will give way as they always do to great exhilaration once the proceedings get underway. And now that moment has arrived. Down on the stage, the curtain is about to rise on the last night of Pageant Week, a night that will end with the coronation of Miss America 1965.[33]

The show now began for the live audience. During the above repartee with the home audience, the Convention Hall Audience could be heard murmuring and talking since they were not privy to any of the above. When asked what the live audience did during commercial breaks, and "color commentary" by the television anchor person, John Koushouris, *Miss America Pageant* producer since 1962, answered, "They just sat there."[34]

The show began (again) with "Come to the Party," and continued as follows:

1. "Come to the Party"
2. Parade of States
3. Presentation of Semi-Finalists
   a) Vicki Powers, Miss Alabama
   b) Vonda Van Dyke, Miss Arizona
   c) Karen Carlson, Miss Arkansas
   d) Leinaala Teruya, Miss Hawaii
   e) Linda Sawyer, Miss Kentucky
   f) Barbara Hasselberg, Miss Minnesota
   g) Jane Nelson, Miss New Mexico
   h) Sharon McCauley, Miss Texas
   i) Lauren Waddleton, Miss Washington
   j) Ella Kessler, Miss West Virginia
4. Presentation of Non-finalist Talent Awards by Lenora Slaughter. They were Most Talented Dancer, Miss Alaska; Best Popular Singer, Miss New York; Best Classical or Semi/classical singer, Miss Colorado; Best Musician, Miss Idaho and Miss Utah (tie); all other categories, Miss Louisiana, Miss Michigan, Miss Virginia.[35]
5. Commercial
6. Introduction of the Judges
7. "Out of Yesterday"
8. Presentation of Miss America 1964
9. Evening Gown Competition
10. Commercial
11. "The Old Soft Shoe"
12. Talent Competition (Commercial/station identification break after the third, sixth, eighth, and tenth contestants)
13. Presentation of Miss Congeniality Award to Miss Arizona, Vonda Kay Van Dyke.
14. "Atlantic City"
15. Swimsuit Competition
16. Commercial
17. "1/3 Old as Methuselah"[36]
18. Announcement of five finalists: At this point, the field of semi-finalists was narrowed down to five finalists. They were: Karen E. Carlson, Miss Arkansas, Ella Dee Kessler, Miss West Virginia, Sharon McCauley, Miss Texas, Barbara P. Hasselberg, Miss Minnesota, and Vonda Van Dyke, Miss Arizona.[37] As each name was announced by Bert Parks, that contestant walked center stage and then stage left where she sat down at one of five seats. Behind these seats stood a male escort dressed in white tie and tails.
19. Interviews: One at a time, in full view of the other contestants, each girl was asked to join Bert Parks center stage for two interview questions.[38] Coming up to the one microphone, each girl, in turn, answered the questions.

20. Commercial
21. Miss America Farewell, speech and song: "May God Keep You in the Palm of His Hand."
22. Commercial
23. Announcement of the four runners-up and Miss America. They were: Fourth Runner-Up, Barbara Hasselberg, Miss Minnesota; Third Runner-Up, Sharon McCauley, Miss Texas; Second Runner-Up Ella Kessler, Miss West Virginia; First Runner-Up, Karen Carlson, Miss Arkansas. As each girl heard her name announced, she left her seat and was taken center stage by an escort. A giant trophy was given to the escort. That girl's chair was taken off, and the remaining seats moved together.

When all the contestants had been called, only one remained, Miss America 1965, Miss Arizona, Vonda Kay Van Dyke. A crown, a cape, a Miss America sash, and a bouquet of flowers was given to the winner as Bert Parks filled in with ad libbed banter. At this point a "gate crasher," identified as Stan Bergman of New York, jumped on stage and tried to give a corsage to the new Miss America. A group of pageant men and guards rushed on stage and shoved him off the stage in full view of Atlantic City and home audiences. Seemingly unruffled, Parks continued his banter. The orchestra took over playing, "Miss America Song." Teary-eyed Miss America 1965 walked down the runway followed by a spotlight and thunderous applause.[39]

To get the Miss America Crown, Vonda Kay Van Dyke worked on every portion of competition from "20 minutes a day in the Arizona sun, to twelve shows a day at a fun park...." When asked whether her preparation was for the judges or for the audience, Van Dyke responded that she played to the judges to win. However, she always kept in mind the audience and the TV cameras, "because win or lose the *public* would build a career in entertainment."[40]

In retrospect, Van Dyke feels that her pageant experience was quite beneficial:

I find I use my research on how to win far more than I've ever used my college degree. The psychology, the attitude, the carriage of a "winner" is something I pull out of my past for everyday life. I believe getting "winning" out of my system when I was young makes me a better wife and mother now. I've had a successful career as a performer, I've taken on selected challenges. I've lived on the "competitive edge." Now I don't need to compete with my husband or daughter and they don't need to compete for my time or energy. I loved my "year," then I adjusted and enjoyed my career. Now I'm very at home, very happy, very satisfied, and thankful.[41]

### 1966 First Color Telecast

John Koushouris, *Miss America Pageant* television producer since 1962, had been the head of CBS's color television experiments since 1945. According to Koushouris, during the early years of color television certain colors, fabrics, and surfaces as well as makeup shades and hair colors had been tested to see how they would appear on screen and for color correction. When putting together the first color telecast of the *Miss America Pageant* Koushouris' experience in the color television field played a part in the choices made for costuming and set designs. Some of those considerations were: avoiding large areas of saturated colors; no earth tones; no dark blues or greens; avoid geometric patterns which cause twinkling or moire effects; avoid white. Former *Miss America Pageant* Executive Vice President John Zerbe recalls that for the first color telecast, men were told to wear light blue shirts because white created "ghost effects."[42] Advances in technology which corrected the white and color balance have eliminated much of the "color taboos" of early color television.

The first *Miss America Pageant* color telecast originated from NBC which, according to Koushouris, had the best color technology and capabilities at the time. Because of this, it was decided that the pageant would best be served by changing networks.[43] From 1966 on the pageant not only would be live from Atlantic City, but Live and in Color.

### Other Changes

The following are some of the other changes in the pageant in the mid to late sixties:

1966    The use of escorts standing behind the five finalists' chairs was stopped.

1967    Lenora Slaughter retired. Albert Marks took over as Executive Director.
        First USO troupe appeared as part of the cast.

1969    "Neat as a Pin Award" ($250) was given to a neat contestant.[44]

# Chapter VIII
## The Seventies:
## Relevancy Knocks and No One Answers

By 1970, the revolution had finally arrived in Atlantic City. Protests on the grounds of sexism and racism were a plenty. To look at the show on television, one would never know it though. Rather than facing the core issues presented by the protestors, the pageant people continued to insist that the pageant was doing the women of America a great favor by offering scholarships. In 1970, another scholarship grant was initiated, the Dr. David B. Allman Medical Scholarship award, for contestants pursuing a career in medicine.[1] Now young beautiful doctors would simply have to don a swim suit and spiked heels to further their career goals. The pageant, further missing the point, sought to modernize the show by adding production numbers that seemed more like feeble attempts by the Geritol Generation at "coolness." These attempts seemed to prove that the producers were making strides to be in tune with the beat of the new generation.

"Being a Miss America during the Vietnam War was not the easiest thing in the world," claims Miss America 1971, Laurel Schaefer. During that time "some thought the concept of Miss America rather frivolous.... Protests at Miss America functions were not uncommon."[2]

As demonstrated above, the pageants of the late sixties and early and mid-seventies were riddled with protest and dissent. Although the early pageants of the nineteen twenties and thirties had been the focus of public protest, the pendulum of public opinion had swung in favor of the pageant in the nineteen forties and fifties. This favorable response was, in part, the result of the efforts of Lenora Slaughter to clean up the image of the pageant by elevating it from a "cheesecake" show to a scholarship pageant. Community support was at its highest during and after the World War Two years.

By the late 1960s the pendulum had swung back. To some it might have been a time of raised consciousness; to others perhaps a time of negative rebellion. Regardless, the pageant once again was, if not reflecting the strains and strides of the times, at least existing in spite of it all.

In 1968, for example, feminist protestors staged a rally against the pageant in front of Convention Hall. Bras, girdles, and "girlie" magazines were burned as a symbol of female liberation. In 1969, the pageant was struck again by protestors claiming that the pageant treated women as sex objects. At one Miss America local preliminary, the 1971 Miss Montclair State College

Pageant (in New Jersey), raw meat was displayed in front of the auditorium. Placards read "Welcome to the Miss Montclair Steak Pageant" or "Meat on Parade."[3]

Although the zealous fervor against the pageant as a symbol of anti-feminist progress had died down somewhat by the 1974 pageant, protest was still clearly evident. Coinciding with the pageant was the convention of NOW, the National Organization of Women. Among the events staged by NOW was a parade of "Wonder Women" chanting, "The hand that rocks the cradle, rocks the boat."[4] Many articles dealing with the confrontation between NOW and the 1974 *Miss America Pageant* participants appeared in various papers throughout the land. The following are examples of these articles: "NOW'll Be Wet During Crowning," *The Press*, September 4, 1974, 14; Constance Barry, "NOW Gets Going," *The Press*, September 7, 1974, 1; Carlo Sardella, " 'Miss America' Faces Ms.," *New York Times*, September 1, 1974, 47 and 54; Judy Klemesrud, "Can Feminists Upstage Miss America?," *New York Times*, September 8, 1974, 58.

Accessibility to the contestants by NOW representatives was non-existent. Although asked to participate in the NOW activities, pageant contestants did not. According to Albert Marks (in the *New York Times*), "It's ridiculous and impossible. The girls are tied up with a demanding schedule...."[5] One NOW conventioneer commented to the *New York Times*, "You know I would like to try to rap with [the contestants]...[b]ut they're impenetrable. They're surrounded by plastic."[6]

Was there any response to the social pressures and changing ways of the 1970s? Perhaps outwardly there wasn't. Comments made by the outgoing and in-coming Miss Americas reflected the 1974 *Miss America Pageant* position on certain feminist concerns. When asked if she felt that the pageant treated women as sex objects, Miss America 1974 Rebecca King responded:

'Sex objects? I'm not sure I even understand what that is...I'm proud of being a woman. I don't feel I'm exploited. I got involved for the scholarship money...which I plan to use this fall at law school. I would never have gotten involved if I thought it was a body-beautiful contest. And after Atlantic City, you never again have to appear in swimsuit.'[7]

Concerning the women's movement, newly crowned Miss America 1975, Shirley Cothran commented to the *New York Times*:

'That is their thing...and this is mine. I respect what they're doing, and hope they can respect me for what I'm doing'.... [Until I get married] [I] prefer 'Miss' Cothran rather than 'Ms.'[8]

The 1974 pageant did, however, make some attempts at modernizing its image. Unlike contestants from earlier pageants, the 1974 *Miss America Pageant* contestants had to answer controversial, issue-oriented questions from the press dealing with topics ranging from rape to prostitution. The 1974 pageant also displayed some anti-racist tolerance. A black contestant, Cheryl Johnson, Miss Wyoming contended for the title of Miss America that year. Less socially important, yet symbolically representative of changing times, the Miss America robe, sash, and roses were, after fifty years, eliminated.[9]

This was the social milieu for the 1974 *Miss America Pageant*. With this in mind, a brief chronology of other changes in the pageants of the 1970s is presented below followed by an in-depth look at the 1974 pageant.

### Changes

Structurally, the 70s pageants became more compact. In 1971, the top five were no longer announced. Miss America and runners-up were selected from a group of ten.[10]

Socially, the pageants of the seventies were insulated enough to not court controversy. As such there was no room for the controversial question or an impromptu dissenting thought on coast-to-coast television. From 1972 until 1988, questions would no longer be asked of the contestants in front of the televised audience. Short rehearsed speeches were made during the evening gown competition.[11]

The pageant people were also wise enough to know that women of the seventies needed to be neither congenial nor neat as a pin to be successful. In 1973, the "Neat as a Pin Award" was messed out of existence. In 1975, the Miss Congeniality award was most politely told to take a hike. After all, what did this award say about the contestants who almost all voted for themselves.[12]

### The 1974 Pageant

The 1974 *Miss America Pageant* began at 8:00 p.m. on Tuesday, September 3, 1974, with the Boardwalk Parade. In 1979, the parade began at Maryland Avenue at the Boardwalk and ended 2.5 miles later at Albany Avenue. At about 9:30 p.m., one and a half hours after the parade's commencement, the skies opened with torrents of rain. Many float-riders opened up see-through umbrellas. Others abandoned the floats and jumped into cars.[13]

The Parade line-up opened with the combined forces of a police motorcycle escort, the United States Army Security Honor Guard and Marching Unit, NAFEC Composite Squadron Ranger Team, and the Atlantic City High School Band. Next to appear were the Grand Marshals Mayor and Mrs. Joseph F. Bradway, Jr., the Mainland Regional High School Band, and the West Deptford Marine Junior ROTC Color Guard Drill Team. Following these came the Miss America Float and the floats carrying the fifty contestants.[14]

Over 150,000 spectators attended the parade which included "smiling beauties, tinsel, waving officials, bikini clad girls, and bands." According to reports, twenty five bands and twenty eight floats were included in the line of march. Among the bands was Iowa's eighty four piece Avoha Hancock Community School Band. This band came to honor one of its former saxophone players, Rebecca King, Miss America, 1974.[15]

Awards were given in the following categories: Grand Prize, Visiting Communities, Banks, Commercial, Public Service, Restaurants, and Entertainment. Forty-five state troopers patrolled the crowds banked on either side of the Boardwalk, until "the deluge slowed to a light rain, which [by then] glistened on rows of empty seats."[16]

### Preliminaries

By 1974, the *Miss America Pageant* had increased its production staff to include a pageant writer/producer/director, George Cavalier, a television producer, John Koushouris, an associate producer/director, Bill Caligari, a choreographer, Peter Gennaro, an assistant choreographer, Marcia Hyland (a local dance teacher), an orchestra leader, an orchestra, and many others. The on-stage cast also increased in number and function. In his twentieth anniversary appearance, the pageant would be again hosted by Bert Parks. This year the pageant would have two on-stage co-hosts, Miss America 1971, Phyllis George and Miss America 1973, Terry Meeuwsen. The "back stage color commentator" was no longer used. Rounding out the cast were: four dancers, a six member "Miss America Chorale," Miss America 1974, Rebecca King, The 1974 Miss America USO Troupe, Miss Louisiana 1973, Debbie Ward, a singer, Kevin Reynolds, and the fifty contestants.

As the cast and staff changed, so did many structural aspects of the program—changes which will be discussed more thoroughly in the final chapter of this book, "Finals." Nevertheless, despite any changes, as in the past, with only slight content variations, the format for the three nights' "shows" was identical.[17]

As in the past, ten finalists were selected during three nights of competition. This selection was based upon points accumulated in the swimsuit, evening gown, and talent competitions held on Wednesday, Thursday, and Friday nights of Pageant week. In addition to these public competitions, private interviews with the judges were held during the afternoon. The judging system for the 1974 *Miss America Pageant* was a bit different than in the 1964 *Miss America Pageant*, however. At the 1974 pageant preliminaries, the contestants were judged based a) 25% on swim suit, b) 25% for on-stage personality, personal interview, and evening gown (a new rule), and c) 50% for talent. The ten contestants with the highest score would be the top ten finalists. For the finals, the three categories of judging were given an equal 33.3% value.[18]

For the preliminaries, the fifty state representatives were divided into three competition groups. On Wednesday, the Mu Group would compete in the evening gown competition, the Alpha Group in the talent competition, and the Sigma Group in the swimsuit competition. On Thursday, the Sigma Group would compete in evening gown, the Mu Group in talent, and the Alpha Group in swimsuit. On the final night of preliminaries, the Alpha Group would compete in evening gown, the Sigma Group would compete in talent, and the Mu Group would compete in swimsuit.[19]

The judges for the 1974 *Miss America Pageant* were

1. Eileen Farrell, opera diva
2. Dr. Wellington B. Gray, Dean at East Carolina University
3. Mary Healy, Actress; Peter Lind Hayes, Entertainer
4. Eddie Foy III, Casting Director
5. Jeanne Meixell, Dance Teacher
6. Colonel Gilbert Mitchell, Music Director for the Northern Virginia Chamber Orchestra
7. Trudy Haynes, Newscaster.[20]

The evenings' programs began each night at 8:30 p.m. with the overture played by the Miss America Orchestra, under the direction of Glen Osser. A drum roll, and four bars of "There She Is" was interrupted by an off stage announcer, later identified as Wayne Howell. Howell gave the audience a cast breakdown. Upon finishing the introduction, the music once again began. This time it was the song "Our Song is a Good Song—Make it Yours." This opening song was sung by the cast members who entered from stage right and left, meeting at center stage. The singing stopped mid-song for a musical interlude. During this interlude, the individual members of the cast were presented to the audience. The final introduction was left for the fifty contestants who came to the stage from the runway. Their entrance was the cue to resume the singing. During this number, various cast members sang solos. The simple, choreographed movements and the shifting of blocking to cover all areas of the stage by the cast animated the production number. At the climax of the number, Bert Parks was introduced. He entered and concluded the musical number with the cast.[21]

The program continued with some light banter between Bert Parks and his two co-hosts. The three shared a stand-up microphone. Next, Parks introduced the fifty contestants by state affiliation, beginning with Miss Wyoming and concluding with Miss Alabama. As each contestant was introduced, each walked to the microphone pre-set center stage. There she stated her name and where her state pageant had been held. To the sounds of clapping hands and light background music, each contestant walked down the runway, and back to the stage.[22]

At this point, the orchestra played the song "Look at Her." Miss America 1974, Rebecca King, was introduced. Making her entrance from the end of the runway, she walked towards the stage, in short diagonals, stopping at each side of the runway intermittently to acknowledge the Convention Hall audience. Next, the judges were introduced.[23]

Next on the program was the evening gown competition production number, "A Good Year." The players in place, the song began, interrupted only for explanation. While the music played, the audience was informed that the next number would incorporate a medley of that year's top musical hits. The production number, indeed, incorporated a potpourri of instrumental, vocal, and dance numbers by soloists or small clusters of performers usually performing center stage. At the close Phyllis George announced that this number had been "only a prelude to our main theme in elegance and beauty." The evening gown competition followed.[24]

For the evening gown competition, each contestant was introduced by name and state affiliation. Each walked center stage to the microphone. At the microphone each stated some personal philosophy or thought. Upon concluding the brief monologue, the contestant would walk a few steps stage right, stop, turn clockwise to show her back to the audience and judges, turn again and walk down and around the runway.[25]

Next came the talent production number, "Brush A Little Sunshine." As in previous numbers, most of the "small cast" production numbers featured soloists or small clusters performing mostly center stage. Costume changes for both the men and women were observed. Small cast production numbers were performed "proscenium" style in front of a curtain. Large cast numbers which included the fifty contestants were performed on the multi-tiered fixed set. The talent competition followed.[26]

The swimsuit competition production number featured the Miss America Dancers and Kevin Reynolds, singer. The swimsuit competition itself featured each contestant walking center stage after her name was announced. Music played in the background, but no narration or talking at all was employed. Reaching center stage, the contestant stopped, turned to show her back, turned again, and walked down the runway. The contestants wore high heeled shoes. The paneled bathing suits worn in the past had been replaced by one piece hip-cut bathing suits. At the 1974, *Miss America Pageant* most contestants wore suits in the red, orange, and pink, families.[27]

The show finished with a production number titled "The House I Live In—This is a Great Country." This number featured Rebecca King, the 1974 USO Troupe, and Debbie Ward, Miss Louisiana 1973. Set on the large glittery fixed set, the production featured solos and group singing. At the climax, the fifty contestants joined in the singing and sang their way down the runway. At the end of the number, the rest of the cast entered to sing a reprise of "Our Song."[28]

The program concluded each night with the announcement of the preliminary swimsuit and talent contest winners. They were:

Wednesday:
    Karen Diane Smith, Miss Kansas, Swimsuit
    Deborah Humphreys Kincaid, Miss Tennessee, Talent
Thursday:
    Shirley Cothran, Miss Texas, Swimsuit
    Darlene Compton, Miss Kentucky, Talent
Friday:
    Lucianne Buchanan, Miss California, Swimsuit
    Jean Ahern, Miss Illinois, Talent

Approximately 7,000 people attended the three nights of preliminary competitions.[29]

*Finals*

Before the culmination of the pageant on Saturday night, months of preparation had taken place. According to reports, planning for the pageant began six months prior. Two weeks before any contestant had arrived in Atlantic City, the scenic artist and the set designer were already busy with their crews assembling the platforms and drops for the 1974 *Miss America Pageant*—"an exciting musical variety show." However, according to Joe Cook, pageant writer, the actual preparation for the pageant began and begins in January of the particular year.[30]

On the Monday before the Saturday telecast, television production units began setting up in Convention Hall for the color telecast. At that time, three mobile units (forty two foot trailers) parked in the "backstage" area of the Hall. These trailers acted as mini-transmission studios. The equipment housed in these trailers along with the seven cameras in Convention Hall had an estimated worth of $1.8 million. The microphones and public address system were estimated to cost $21,000.[31]

Workers from the local Brotherhood of Electrical Workers rigged the electrical wires and lamps used in lighting the set. The lighting equipment was rented from New York companies for approximately $68,000. Local lighting people ran the lights.[32]

In addition to the above expenses, $127,500 was spent on mounting the production (sets, costumes, and so forth). $400,000 was paid to NBC to broadcast the show, and $90,000 was budgeted to pay the pageant and television producers, Bert Parks, the choreographer, "and others." Unlike pre-television *Miss America Pageants*, funding did not come from the gate receipts. The bill for televised *Miss America Pageants* was paid by the national sponsors.[33]

The months of preparation and planning, the large budget, and professional talent could not in themselves assure a high caliber show. Also needed was rehearsal time. According to Miss New Jersey 1980, Therese Hanley, the contestants rehearse not only for the production numbers, but also for the competition numbers. A "mock" coronation is even staged so that in the event a contestant is chosen Miss America, she will know exactly what to do.[34] The need to please the television audience more than the Convention Hall audience might be verified, in part, by the use of the preliminary audiences, to some degree, as "guinea pigs." Although daytime rehearsals for the show's many aspects were conducted, the three nights of preliminary competitions were, in essence, used as dress rehearsal for the Saturday night finals. During the preliminaries, the show was "de-bugged" of any mistakes, glitches, or slow pacing. At the preliminaries, the production staff also got a chance to plot out camera angles and other telecast considerations. A lengthy television rehearsal held during the day also helped to assure a slick production. To assure that there are no unforeseen glitches, according to pageant writer, Joe Cook, everything is scripted and rehearsed from the first hello. Even the "turns" during competition segments are timed. Although it is unknown exactly how many pages the 1974 script held, the

1986 pageant, to give an example, consisted of one hundred and two pages of script. According to Cook, there is little room for improvisation.[35]

Another example of how the live audience was treated as second rate at worst, or as part of the show at best, was in its subjection to viewing the repetition of the same show's activities in one night. As in the 1964 pageant, the live audience at Convention Hall experienced two shows. The "first show" began at 8:30 p.m. and lasted until 10:00 p.m. when the nationwide telecast was broadcast to NBC television stations throughout the country. At this point the entire show would commence from the beginning. This "second show" was seen both by the Convention Hall Audience and by home viewers in its two hour run. The 1974 *Miss America Pageant* would receive a 30.3 rating and a 57 share of the audience.[36]

According to the pageant program, the 1974 *Miss America Pageant* finals began at 8:30 p.m. with the overture. From here the program followed the preliminary night pageant's format (with a few variations). Unlike the 1964 *Miss America Pageant*, however, there were no competition events during this pre-television show. Neither were the semi-finalists announced. According to the pageant program, the content was as follows: a) "Our Song is a Good Song—Make It Yours," b) "Look At Her," c) "Spotlight on Runway," d) Presentation of Parade Awards, e) Divertissement, f) Introductions, g) Divertissement, h) Intermission.[37]

At this point, according to the pageant program, "at 10 P.M. the Nationwide Color Telecast begins over NBC-TV." As in the 1964 *Miss America Pageant*, for the benefit of the television audiences, the program began all over again. At 10:00 p.m., home viewers saw the NBC peacock, and heard a voice-over: "The following program is brought to you in living color on NBC. Some of the audio and non-contestant video has been pre-recorded for technical quality." According to both Joe Cook and John Koushouris, the pageant has prided itself in being one of the truly all live telecasts left on television.[38]

This portion of the program began with spotlights combing the audience at Convention Hall. The first four bars of "Look At Her" were played by the orchestra. Next a drum roll was heard interrupting the music. Bert Parks, in actuality backstage, appeared on the screen superimposed against the Convention Hall setting.[39] He spoke: "Good evening, I'm Bert Parks. You know, over the years we've enjoyed some exciting moments together. Moments like these." Bert's image dissolved. In its place, the home audience was shown highlights of recent Miss America crownings. Although future Miss America audiences at Convention Hall could see the television images on a giant screen at the Hall, according to John Koushouris, this was not implemented until 1982.

After this brief introduction, the show, as in the preliminaries, once again began with the introduction of the cast. The action proceeded with "Our Song." While the dancers danced on stage, the home audience saw the commercial sponsors' logos superimposed on the screen. A voice-over gave brief commercial promotions for each sponsor's product.[40] The production number continued with the entrance of the fifty contestants. It ended the same as in the preliminaries. After the fifty contestants were introduced, the action was halted for two commercials. All commercials were introduced by one of the former Miss America co-hosts. For this introduction, they spoke directly into a camera to the home audience.

After the commercial break, Miss America 1974 was introduced as Parks sang "Look At Her." Next on the program was the announcement of the ten semi-finalists. Parks explained to the audience the process involved in selecting the semi-finalists. As Parks read off each name, the orchestra would punctuate the "tension" with some modulating chords. Each contestant chosen as a semi-finalist walked center stage forming a straight line down stage. When the last contestant was named, the orchestra resolved its musical fanfares. The contestants walked off stage right as the orchestra played. The top ten were:

1. Miss Tennessee, Deborah Humphreys Kincaid
2. Miss Illinois, Jean Ahern
3. Miss New Mexico, Donna Reel
4. Miss Kentucky, Darlene Compton
5. Miss Texas, Shirley Cothran
6. Miss South Dakota, Barbara Marie Guthmiller
7. Miss Louisiana, Libby Lovejoy
8. Miss Indiana, Penny Tichenor
9. Miss California, Lucianne Buchanan
10. Miss Washington, Kathleen Beth Moore[41]

The judges were introduced, and the action was again suspended for two commercials.[42] After the commercial break, Bert Parks introduced *Miss America Pageant* Executive Director, Albert Marks. Marks, standing in the audience, looked into the camera and said the following:

...We hope you're enjoying our show tonight. But, let's face it, no matter who is selected among the fifty to wear the crown of Miss America, there will always be those who think it should have been someone else. It's an impossible task at best. The truth is any girl between eighteen and twenty-eight who has never been married can enter the Miss America Pageant, and any of the fifty finalists can win it. But please remember, this is not a beauty contest, although beauty is important. This is not a popularity contest, although personality is equally important. This is not a talent show, although each girl is scored on her talent performance. All three competitions, evening gown, swimsuit, and talent play a part in the accumulation of points by the contestants as does a part of the pageant you don't see. You don't see the interviews with the judges which is considered a part of the evening gown competition.

When our ten finalists start tonight, their previous points are not considered except in case of a tie. The judges, in selecting Miss America means finding a girl not just for a single night in the limelight, but a girl with qualities that will carry her through a full year of difficult and varied assignments.

Incidentally, even the judges don't know who's won until the votes are tabulated and their decision announced by Bert Parks. We hope this makes the judging procedure a little clearer for you in the audience. Now let's get on with the show.[43]

The above speech was given, in part, in accordance with broadcast laws. According to Joe Cook, *Miss America Pageant* writer, as per FCC Broadcast Standards of Compliance, the rules for the *Miss America Pageant* must be stated at some point during the telecast.[44]

Besides the above reason, another reason for this disclaimer might have been to justify the selection process. According to Frank Deford, the previous year's selection, Rebecca King, was booed because of the Convention Hall audience's displeasure with that selection.[45]

The show continued as follows:

a) Introduction of New Jersey Governor Byrnes

b) "It Was a Very Good Year"

c) Evening gown competition

d) Two commercials

e) "Brush a Little Sunshine"

f) Talent competition

g) "Travelin' Prayer"

h) Swimsuit Competition

i) Announcement of Miss Congeniality: Miss Arkansas, Rhonda Kay Pope and Miss Hawaii, Coline Helen Kaualoku Aiu (Tie).

j) Announcement of talent awards. For this announcement, the girl who won stepped forward from the ranks of the other fifty contestants. The announcement of each name was punctuated musically. For the 1974 *Miss America Pageant* no individual categories, *i.e.*, best dancer, were selected.

k) Introduction of Miss America 1924, Ruth Malcolmson. The former Miss America walked down the runway to a standing ovation. A split screen showed Miss America 1924 walking on one side and a wide-eyed little girl in the audience on the other.

l) Two commercials

m) Production number by U.S.O. Troupe

n) Two Commercials

o) Miss America Farewell. Rebecca King walked down the runway as the orchestra played "Miss America You're Beautiful." Bert Parks sang the lyrics. As she walked down the runway, a pre-recorded tape of King's voice was played. The content of this tape basically expressed her sentiments on being Miss America.[46]

At this point, the action differed from the preliminaries. It also differed from the previous *Miss America Pageants* discussed in prior chapters. The practice of narrowing down the ten semi-finalists to five finalists was no longer in effect. Instead, the ten finalists stood in a straight line at the stage left apron. An off-stage voice (female) reminded the audience who each of the ten finalists was. Before the announcement of the winner, there was a pause for another commercial.[47]

The moment to announce Miss America 1975 was held back by a silent last look at the contestants.[48] A drum roll began before each runner-up was announced. After each name was announced, a musical tag to build suspense was played. The runners-up were: Fourth Runner-up, Libby Lovejoy, Miss Louisiana; Third Runner-up, Darlene Compton, Miss Kentucky; Second Runner-up, Jean Ahern, Miss Illinois; First Runner-Up, Lucianne Buchanan, Miss California. Miss America's name was then announced. She was Miss Texas, Shirley Cothran. The robe, sash, and roses of yesteryear had been abandoned. A tiara was pinned to her hair and a scepter was handed to her. As this ritual was taking place, the following "filler" dialogue took place:[49]

Bert Parks: Shirley Cothran, Miss Texas—What city in Texas?
Shirley Cothran: Fort Worth.
Bert: Fort Worth—Shirley, how does it [the crown] fit? Alright?
Shirley: It feels fine.
Bert: It looks beautiful on you.
Shirley: Thank you.
Bert: Think it'll hold? Yours [Rebecca King] fell off, I think. (*To Shirley*) Have you ever—
        did you ever dream of this moment?
Shirley: No-o-o—I don't know how you can ask me questions at a time like this.
Bert: Let's greet our new Miss America. Here we go. There is America waiting for you.

Bert Parks sang the "Miss America Song" as Shirley Cothran, Miss America 1975 walked down the runway. As she did so, the runners-up walked up the platform stairs set center stage. So doing, they flanked the throne on which Cothran would sit. The other contestants stood frozen to their pre-blocked positions. During this time the audience at Convention Hall stood and applauded. The audience still watching at home saw the sponsor logos super-imposed over the live action. The announcer reminded the home audience who had sponsored the show. The credits rolled, and the 1974 *Miss America Pageant* was over.[50] Outside, the First Amendment of the Republic had been freely exercised. Inside, the Miss America monarchy had crowned its newest queen.

# Chapter IX
## The Eighties, The Scandals

The early 1980s was a time of both scandal and purging. At times the purging and the scandals were married. When they were not, the attempts to clean house seemed to be based on the familiar philosophy "out with the old and in with the new."

First runner-up in the category of most notorious change of the eighties was the firing of Bert Parks as host. In 1980 Bert Parks was replaced by actor Ron Ely as master of ceremony after twenty-five years of faithful service.[1] According to Albert Marks, the pageant sponsors had been pressuring him to get rid of the "aging Bert" for twelve years. This firing of Bert Parks because of his age prompted an on-air campaign by Johnny Carson on the *Tonight Show*.[2]

Ely's tenure would be a short one. Though his departure did not receive as much notoriety as Parks', in 1982, Ely too was axed. He was replaced by television personality and husband of former Miss America, Mary Ann Mobley, Gary Collins. Also taking its farewell walk in the eighties was the Miss America Troupe who tapped its way out of the pageant after the 1980 telecast. In 1982, the position of television co-host was also abolished. With this change, the pageant people admitted what America already knew: the pageant was entertainment, not news. Former Miss Americas would henceforth do the commercial lead-ins.[3] Finally, the winner in the (not too) fond farewells department was Vanessa Williams, who all by herself brought both fame and infamy to the pageant.

### The Vanessa Williams Scandal

In 1983, the first black Miss America, Vanessa Williams was selected. The first runner-up, Suzette Charles, was also black. This was historical indeed. According to Atlantic City writer Mary Flanagan, "The pageant was lily white until 1970 when Cheryl Browne of Iowa became the first black to appear on stage [as a contestant]."[4]

History would be made again. In July of 1984, *Penthouse* magazine publisher Bob Guccione announced that nude photographs of Vanessa Williams would be published in the magazine. When published, the cover of the magazine showed Williams with actor George Burns. The headlines read, "Oh, God, She's Nude." The magazine featured black and white pictures of Vanessa Williams in frontal nudity poses. Other photos showed Williams posing in sexual positions with another woman identified as Amy Geier.

These photos appeared in both the "Oh, God" issue in September and in another *Penthouse* issue in November. Still another set of photos would surface in January's edition of *Penthouse* by a different photographer. These photos showed Williams in sado-masochistic positions and costumes, *i.e.*, leather straps, harnesses, handcuffs. The cover headline for this pictorial spread was "Oh, God, I Did It Again."[5] When the first set of photos surfaced, *Miss America Pageant* Director Al Marks said he would strip Williams of her title if she did not resign. She did. First runner-up Suzette Charles was named Miss America 1984.[6]

Commentary for and against Williams, the pageant, Guccione, and others saturated the air waves and news stands. The literature on the scandal (or the "incident") is voluminous. Among the articles: Robin Morgan, "The Vanessa Williams Controversy: What's a Feminist to Think?," *Ms.* October 1984: 154; Peter McLaughlin and Stuart Marques, "Vanessa Set to Fess Up," *The [New York] Daily News (New York Daily News)* July 22, 1984: 5; Ellen Goodman, "Miss America Paid the Price For Crossing the Line Between Pageantry and Pornography," *The Hudson [New Jersey] Dispatch* July 31, 1984: 11; "There She Goes—Miss America is Told to Quit," *New York Daily News* July 21, 1984: 1; "Miss America Exposed: Vanessa the Undressa," *New York Daily News* July 21, 1984: 21; Stuart Marques, "Whooosh!—Miss America Ducks Press on Her Return," *New York Daily News* July 21, 1984: 3; Peter Moses and Larry Nathanson, "Favorite Daughter Still Reigns in Home Town," *New York Post* July 21, 1984: 3.

Public interest (or curiosity) in the pageant boomed. According to Marks, by the beginning of pageant week, ticket sales were up 20% from the previous year. By Monday of Pageant Week, the Saturday night finals were sold out.[7] In 1983 about three hundred and fifty press representatives had covered the pageant. The majority showed up on the final day of pageant week. By Monday, September 10, 1984, over four hundred media representatives had already swarmed to Atlantic City. Represented were *The New York Times*, *The Los Angeles Times*, *The Boston Herald*, *USA Today*, *Newsweek*, *Essence*, *Rolling Stone* and local papers from all over the country. In addition, over a dozen television news teams from the United States, England, and Germany, were on hand to cover the pageant activities. Two groups protested the pageant, "Women Against Pornography" and "Females for Felons."[8]

In 1984, a month after "the incident," just when everyone thought it was safe and all things were in order, scandal once more stuck its eely fingers into the eyes of the pageant. The Vanessa scandal would not be the only dark cloud looming over the 1984 pageant. News leaked out that Miss Ohio, Melissa Bradley, had been arrested for shoplifting in 1982. Bradley was not disqualified from the pageant because the charges had been dropped.[9]

The 1984 pageant would begin under tense conditions indeed. Questions were raised: "Would 'they' mention 'her' name on the air?" "How would 'they' handle 'it'?" "What were 'they' going to tell 'them'?" "What would happen if 'she' won?"

With bated breath America waited for these and other answers. With head held high, the 1984 pageant went on. Having survived the Williams incident, everything else was a piece of cake. When asked about the scandal, the pageant had a rehearsed and pat answer that would transcend the verbal into the realm of attitude: "The pageant has not suffered. Only Vanessa has."[10]

### The 1984 Pageant

#### The Boardwalk Parade

The aura of scandal surrounding the pageant was not the only concern of its organizers in the pageant after the incident. Other factors seemed to be impeding the success of one traditional aspect of the *Miss America Pageant*, the Boardwalk Parade. Because of the outdoor nature of parades, in general, bad weather can cause the cancellation or ruination of a parade. This had been the case for the Boardwalk Parade. It had been thwarted by rain for the previous five years.[11]

Other more serious threats to the parade's continuation were the increasing production costs and the diminishing attendance. These two factors caused *Miss America Pageant* officials to consider its cancellation in 1983. Just the opposite occurred. The fifty-sixth annual parade became larger in number of participants and in production scale. Parade chairperson Ellen Greenspan speculated to *The [Atlantic City] Press* that the parade would be 10% larger than the previous year's. There would be one hundred twenty-one units involved with approximately 3,600 people participating. The numbers were increased by the addition of six more marching bands and five more floats. A total of twenty-one bands would appear in the parade. Included in this roster of bands were seventeen high school bands from all over the country, four string bands, one full orchestra, and a "hobo band." Also adding to the increase in participants by one was the fifty-first *Miss America Pageant* contestant, Miss District of Columbia.[12]

The parade featured a float sponsored by the Atlantic City Casino Organization. This float was hailed as one of the largest in any parade. It rested on four flat-bed trailers and carried the Paul Mann Orchestra. Another novel feature of the parade was the inclusion of a live camel. The contestants would ride in Renault Alliance Convertibles.[13]

The parade began at 8:30 p.m. at New Jersey Avenue and ended at Albany Avenue two and one-half miles later. Over two hundred thousand people lined each side of the Boardwalk.[14] These spectators either stood for free, or sat on grandstand or bleacher seats set up along the Boardwalk. Grandstand seats were $6.50 and bleacher seats cost $3.

An innovation in the parade organization was the creation of a command center. The command center was operated by eight members of the parade committee from within Convention Hall. This committee monitored the flow of the parade based upon information relayed to them via two-way radios by members of the SCARA Ham Radio Club. These club members patrolled the parade on foot. Parade volunteers filled gaps in the parade where there were spaces and pauses. Members of the parade committee also saw that parade participants quickly disbanded at the end of the parade route so that there would be no bottlenecking or unnecessary stalling.[15]

By 1984, two "off-beat" and unofficial habits had become a part of the interchange between the parade participants and the audience. One "ritual" was the "hog calling" (for want of a better title); the other, "show us your shoes." The first, hog calling, was a yearly tradition of the Arkansas contingency. In honor of the state's "razorback" nickname, the Arkansas delegation stood in front of Convention Hall and made hog calls. In 1984, two men dressed in hog costumes led the chants.[16]

The second tradition, "show us your shoes," began in the late 1970s. According to Virginia Mann, writing in *The Record* [New Jersey], this started in 1978. Because of their vantage point, seventeen men watching the parade from a New York Avenue hotel balcony could look into the cars driving by. They noticed what ground-level audiences could not see. Some contestants were wearing slippers. They shouted: "Show us your shoes."[17]

There is another variation to how this tradition started. During the parades of the mid-1970s, a local transvestite, called Tinsel Garland, would crash the parade rank and files dressed as Dorothy from the Wizard of Oz. The crowd would yell out, "Show us your shoes," as in ruby red slippers. Tinsel Garland stopped crashing the parades, but the tradition stuck. Each year the gay bars along New York Avenue throw "show us your shoes" parties. As the contestants ride by New York Avenue, the revelers cry, "Show us your shoes." *Miss America Pageant* contestants lift their gowns to show ski boots, bed room slippers, fins, and other types of shoes. The contestant that refuses to show her shoes gets booed and jeered at by the crowd.[18]

The 1984 parade was not completely tension-free. Numerous calls and letters to the *Miss America Pageant* headquarters had been received, threatening the lives of the six black contestants. Two hundred twenty police combed the area for security purposes. One hundred were from Atlantic City and eighty from other areas. City police officers riding motorcycles flanked Suzette Charles' float. Fire fighter teams and first aid squads were also on hand to provide safety.[19]

The parade lasted about two hours. The Grand Marshals for the 1984 parade were A. Martinez, Stephen Schnetzer, and Martin Vidnovic, three soap opera personalities. Awards were given to floats in the following categories: a) Grand Sweepstakes, b) Best Overall Effect, c) Non-commercial Division, d) Commercial Division. Three high school bands were awarded first, second, and third prizes—Miss America flags.[20]

*Preliminaries*

Changes in the *Miss America Pageant* preliminaries between 1974 and 1984 were few. For the most part, the *Miss America Pageant*, as a combination variety show and contest, retained its basic form. There would be three nights of preliminary competitions. The three preliminary night competitions would again consist of three groups of contestants in competing in evening gown, swimsuit, and talent on alternate nights.

The entertainment portion of the *Miss America Pageant* likewise retained its song-and-dance variety show format. The titles of the songs might have been different, but the basic "formula," with slight variations, remained relatively the same as the following demonstrates:[21]

a) overture

b) full cast production number

c) parade of states

d) Miss America walk

e) introduction of judges

f) production number before the swimsuit competition

g) swimsuit competition: The swimsuit competition, usually left for last, was changed to the first element of competition for the 1984 pageant. According to John Koushouris in his interview with the investigator, the swimsuit competition had been last in previous years because of its audience popularity. Anticipation and expectation would build up. Koushouris suggests that in the post-Vanessa atmosphere, placing the swimsuit competition first would de-emphasize its importance and impact.[22]

h) production number before talent competition

i) talent competition

j) production number before the evening gown competition

k) evening gown competition

l) full cast production number/reprise of theme

m) selection of preliminary winners in swim suit and talent

The creative team for the 1984 *Miss America Pageant* also remained the same as in 1974. Major staff positions, *i.e.*, producer, writer, choreographer and orchestra leader, both for the live pageant and the televised pageant, were held by the same people.

Changes in the size and make-up of the cast were evident. Bert Parks had been replaced by Gary Collins as host. Like the 1974 pageant, two former Miss Americas were part of the cast. This year they were Miss America 1982, Elizabeth Ward and Miss America 1983, Debra Maffett. The on-stage cast also included the Miss America Dancers. The number of dancers had doubled from four to eight. The voices of the Miss America Chorale were heard on tape. There was no U.S.O. troupe or any former contestants in the 1984 cast. Featured instead were three current soap opera stars, A. Martinez, Stephen Schnetzer and Martin Vidnovic.[23]

The judges for the 1984 *Miss America Pageant* were: Rebecca King, Miss America 1974; Leroy Nieman, Sports Artist; Pearl Bailey, Entertainer; Josiah Bunting, III, President, Hampden-Sydney College; Vivian Blaine, Actress; Sam Haskell, Talent Executive, William Morris Agency; Chris Little, Freelance Photographer; and Dixie Ross Neill, Opera Diva.[24]

Although the preliminaries offered the Convention Hall audience pre-pageant entertainment, the pageant itself began at 8:15 p.m. with the overture played by the Miss America Orchestra, under the direction of Glen Osser.

Preliminaries lasted approximately two hours each night. The program for the preliminary competitions was identical to that of finals with minor exceptions.[25]

The program concluded each night with the announcement of the preliminary swimsuit and talent contest winners. They were:

Wednesday:
> Tamara Hext, Miss Texas, Swimsuit
> Margaret Marie O'Brien, Miss Massachusetts, Talent

Thursday:
> Sharlene Wells, Miss Utah, Swimsuit
> Mary-Ann Farrell, Miss New York, Talent

Friday:
> Kathy Manning, Miss Mississippi, Swimsuit
> Lauren Susan Green, Miss Minnesota, Talent

Approximately 9,000 people attended on Wednesday; 11,000 on Thursday; 13,000 on Friday.[26]

*Finals*

In televised pageants discussed previously, the Saturday night show had started, in actuality, before the television cameras picked up the action at 10:00 p.m. The same show would be repeated at that time. By 1984, this procedure had been abandoned. The Convention Hall audience attended a pre-television show from 9:00 p.m. to 9:30 p.m. This show contained live song and dance entertainment. From 9:30 to 10:00 there was an intermission.[27] At 10:00 p.m. a completely different show began. This show, the Saturday night finals of the 1984 *Miss America Pageant*, was the same in content and format as the preliminaries with a few content exceptions.

The show began with Miss America 1984, Suzette Charles, introducing each state contestant from her position at the end of the runway. Two microphones were set on the stage. Beginning with Miss Alabama, each contestant would step to one of the two empty microphones and state her name and her school affiliation. By having two microphones, the speed and flow of the action was uninterrupted. In previous pageants one microphone was used. Each contestant had to wait until the microphone was available upon the previous contestant's departure. After each contestant had finished with her introduction, the contestant walked down and around the 120-foot, foot-lighted runway.[28]

When the last contestant had been introduced, the live action switched to video tape. This video tape showed a series of Atlantic City attractions flipping, wiping, and dissolving on the screen. Attractions included the beach, hotels, and fireworks. The song "On the Boardwalk in Atlantic City" played in the background. By 1984 two giant screens had been placed next to the stage above the Convention Hall crowds. All of the action seen by the home television audiences, including commercials, could be seen by the live audience. An announcer said the following:

*Voice Over*

From the Boardwalk in Atlantic City, the most famous main street in America. The new Atlantic City, getting newer every year. Where 26 million people every year make it the most visited resort city in the world. Atlantic City—where the great stars shine at spectacular entertainment centers. Romantic, enchanting, Atlantic City, home of the Miss America pageant for over sixty years. Miss America—the most imitated pageant in the world. This is the original. Tonight young women from every state and the District of Columbia will compete for scholarships in the most prestigious pageant of all. Now live from Convention Hall, the Miss America Pageant.[29]

At this point, the action switched back to live. Spotlights flooded the stage. A colorfully lit cyclorama spanned the back wall of the stage. The announcer continued his monologue by introducing the cast. Names were superimposed on the screen. As he spoke, the music continued in the background. Shots of the audience from all angles were captured by the cameras. The orchestra, on stage, was featured on screen. At this point, the music picked up and the dancers entered the stage area. They danced briefly to the music. As the dancers danced off the stage, the contestants entered the stage area "lip syncing" the 1984 pageant's theme song, "Maybe It's Your Turn Now." According to John Koushouris, in the past microphone and other forms of audio trouble left some of the performers disgruntled.[30] The pre-taped music insured a smooth performance. The announcer's voice announced the commercial sponsors' names. On the television screens (telecast and in Convention Hall) the sponsors' logos were superimposed over the on-stage choreographed movement.

The announcer next re-introduced the cast. This time during the introductions, each cast member walked center stage, bowed to the camera, and walked off stage left (screen right). During this time all areas of the stage and runway were busy with motion and action. The song concluded and Gary Collins said a few words of introduction. The show had begun— but first a word from the sponsors. For the most part each commercial break consisted of two thirty-second commercials. During the commercial break, the live audience sat and watched the commercials on the big screen.[31]

The next event on the program was the introduction of Suzette Charles to the audience. As in 1974, the reigning Miss America appeared at the end of the runway and zig-zagged her way to the stage, stopping at the end of each diagonal to wave to a different side of the audience. For this walk, Gary Collins "sang" "Miss America You're Beautiful." The Convention Hall audience rose to its feet and applauded.[32]

The announcement of the ten semi-finalists was at hand. First, the general rules and procedures were told to the audience. This rather potentially tedious discourse took the form of a brief, light-hearted conversation between Gary Collins and Debbie Maffett. For this introduction, Collins and Maffett carried cordless microphones.[33] The envelope containing the names of the semi-finalists was already in Gary Collins' pocket. According to John Koushouris, the selection of the ten semi-finalists is made after the Friday night preliminary. According to *Miss America Pageant* Press Chairperson, Jean Bray, the press is given the names of the top ten a few hours before the beginning of the Saturday night finals.[34] They were:

1. Miss Massachusetts, Margaret Marie O'Brien
2. Miss Texas, Tamara Hext
3. Miss Minnesota, Lauren Susan Green
4. Miss Kentucky, Kelly Brumagen
5. Miss Hawaii, Debbie Nakanelua
6. Miss Ohio, Melissa Bradley
7. Miss New York, Mary-Ann Farrell
8. Miss Mississippi, Kathy Manning
9. Miss Utah, Sharlene Wells
10. Miss Tennessee, Shelley Mangrum

As each contestant was announced, the same fanfare was played as in the 1974 pageant. The contestants formed a straight line at the apron of the stage. When the final contestant was named, all the contestants left the stage. The curtain then closed.[35]

The judges were announced by Gary Collins. As each judge was announced, he or she stood from their box seat in the orchestra pit, and bowed to the audience. On screen, the judges names were superimposed. After the introduction of the judges, Miss New York, 1970, Doctor Katharine Karlsrud, spoke briefly of how she had benefitted from the *Miss America Pageant* scholarships. She then announced the winner of the Dr. David B. Allman Award for a contestant pursuing a medical career. That contestant was Miss Kentucky, Kelly Brumagen. Next there was a commercial break.[36]

After the commercial break, Gary Collins, wearing a different tuxedo than in the last scene, introduced the next production number. This number featured the soap opera stars and the former and current Miss Americas: "Let's Hear it for the Boy." At the end of the number, a commercial break was announced. A shot of one of the finalists appeared on the screens. This contestant said a small blurb ending with "Maybe it's my turn now" (the theme of the show) before every commercial. This would be repeated by different semi-finalists throughout the show. The swimsuit competition would follow after the commercial. Two commercials later, the cameras returned briefly to Convention Hall for the announcement of station identification. Two local commercials and three sponsor commercials followed.[37]

For the swimsuit competition, the contestants walked down a flight of stairs set on the stage as her name and state affiliation was announced by Collins. Many of the contestants were observed on video tape and live to be wearing original (or facsimile) white Ada Duckett super suits. This swimsuit "custom-engineered" by seamstress Ada Duckett is tailor-made for the contestant's specific body type. It is recognizable by its style and cut. Those contestants walked in a diagonal, stage left. Music played in the background. As she walked, a split screen viewable by both home and

Convention Hall audiences, showed a brief excerpt of the contestants' interviews earlier that week with the judges. After stopping in front of the judges, the contestants proceeded down and around the runway.[38] A commercial break followed.

The next number introduced by Gary Collins (in a different tuxedo) featured Suzette Charles and the Miss America Dancers—"Music is My Way of Life." The talent competition followed.[39]

For the talent competition, two contestants performed followed by a commercial break. Those contestants using microphones used cordless microphones. Behind the contestants, different patterns or colors on the cyclorama complemented the performance.

According to John Koushouris, the contestants rehearse during the day for their talent segments. During this time not only are the musical and audio glitches smoothed over, but also the visuals. The production staff has a chance to see what will look the best scenically and electrically based on the type of number, color of the costume, and other factors. In some instances, camera shots were taken from behind the girl, showing the audience. The Convention Hall audience, in essence, became a part of the content of the show, as they watched themselves on the giant screens. At the end of the performance, the woman's image was captured and frozen on the screen. Superimposed on this image was her name, state affiliation, college, and age.[40]

The next production number attempted to be humorous. According to Albert Marks in *The [Atlantic City] Press*, "We're trying to lighten up the show because of the heavy aspects of what happened this summer." The "satirical" number featured the soap opera stars and the former and reigning Miss Americas in color-coordinated costumes.[41]

The evening gown competition followed. For this competition, each contestant again walked down a staircase as she was announced by Gary Collins. Music accompanied the walk. Walking in a diagonal direction stage left, each contestant stopped in front of the judges. Her state name was flashed on the screen. Speaking into a stand-up microphone, the contestant stated a brief, memorized, personal philosophy. Finishing her speech she turned to show the back of her gown, turned again, and walked down and around the runway. A commercial break followed.[42]

The final production number featured everyone in the cast including the fifty contestants. Basically, the number, "Best of Times," featured small groups or soloists singing a few bars from the song center stage. Eventually, the complete cast entered the stage area. The contestants and cast marched onto the stage and worked their way down the runway. The dancers danced on the stage waving large flags. The production number climaxed musically and visually on the runway. To get the cast back on stage, the theme "Maybe It's Your Turn" was reprised. A commercial break followed.[43]

After the break the non-finalist talent awards were announced. As Gary Collins announced each winner, that woman stepped forward on stage. On screen, a clip of her performance was shown. Next on the program was

Miss America's farewell. Gary Collins introduced Suzette Charles. With tiara on her head, Charles walked down the runway waving at the audience. Collins sang the first few bars of "Miss America You're Beautiful." In the middle of Collins' singing, he stopped. Scenes from last year's pageant—the parade and competition segments—appeared on a split screen. A taped speech made by Charles was played. After the speech, her voice could be heard singing her talent competition number from the 1983 pageant—"Kiss Me in the Rain." The audience stood applauding. By the time the tape and visual images had finished, Suzette Charles had returned to the stage. A commercial break followed.[44]

After the commercial break, the ten finalists appeared standing in a straight line. Gary Collins re-introduced each finalist by name. The camera worked its way slowly down this line stopping at each girl. As it did, a split screen showed the contestant live on one side, and the contestant in the three competitions that night. A commercial break followed.[45]

At this point, Gary Collins crossed to the judges for the envelope containing the winners' names. The unexpected happened—the judges were not ready. For the following minutes an embarrassed Collins improvised with Suzette Charles. The conversation rambled. Collins joked, "What would Bert [Parks] do in this situation?" The judges still were not ready. Suzette Charles talked about her future plans. The judges finally handed the decision to a relieved Collins. The finalists were:[46]

1. Fourth runner-up, Miss Texas, Tamara Hext
2. Third runner-up, Miss Minnesota, Lauren Susan Green
3. Second runner-up, Miss Mississippi, Kathy Manning
4. First runner-up, Melissa Bradley, Miss Ohio
5. Miss America 1985, Sharlene Wells, Miss Utah

As each finalist was announced, she went center stage. The line of girls holding hands closed in. When Miss America was announced, the five remaining contestants hugged and kissed her. Suzette Charles pinned the tiara on her head. The tiara had tape on the center to hold it down on the winner's head. She was handed a scepter with flowers on it, and seconds later, she was walking down the runway as Collins "sang" a new coronation song—"Look at Her." The traditional song, "The Miss America Song" ("There She Is") was not used because of royalty disagreements between composer, Bernie Wayne, and the *Miss America Pageant* organization.[47]

As the new Miss America returned to the stage, Collins bade the audiences good-bye until next year. Reaching the stage, the Miss America 1985 was "mobbed" by contestant well-wishers. They kissed the new Miss America and milled around her. While this happened on stage, the sponsors' logos were supered on the screen, the announcer stated these sponsors' names, the music played, the credits rolled, and the spotlights combed the audience which, en route out of Convention Hall, was no longer paying attention to the screens.[48]

The new Miss America was a Mormon. The press emphasized her conservative social and political views and her "squeaky clean" image.[49] Some of her views on the pageant are quite candid and straightforward. She writes:

> Those of us competing have (and had) an idealistic view of the program—we were in it because of the scholarship, the opportunity to show our talents, etc. In a way, not idealistic at all. But as I have been through my reign and reflect on the many attitudes I encountered, I see that those watching the pageant on the *outside* (even those intimately involved as directors, hostesses, producers), many of those still see this as a "cattle call"— a way to promote "their girl" over the "other girls" by merely comparing those attributes only displayed on stage. The Miss A. pageant is not a beauty pageant in the eyes of us who knew it as *one* way to achieve other goals....[50]

### In Conclusion (Almost): Then 'Til Now

From then 'til now, the pageant has changed little. As far as scandals, the tabloids unearthed that a member of Miss America 1986 Susan Akin's family was somehow connected to the killing of Mississippi's Freedom Fighters. True or untrue, just or unjust, the pageant used to scandal by now was unruffled by all of it and simply shrugged the whole thing off.

In another scandal, in 1985, Miss New Jersey, Toni Georgiana, made national news when first runner-up, Laura Bridges, filed a law suit against the Miss New Jersey Pageant. Bridges claimed that Georgiana actually lived in Pennsylvania, and further, that she was not truly a New Jersey student since she was enrolled in only one never-attended course at Trenton State College in New Jersey. Bridges claimed that Georgiana, in view of the above, was not a *bona fide*, Miss New Jersey. Bridges lost the case, but brought into focus the common practice of state-hopping (or crown chasing). More importantly, the incident raised the question of the validity of scholarship in the pageant when the dubious practice of enrolling for and never attending a course was commonplace among non-collegiate pageant hopefuls. Such scholarship recipients have used their money for private vocal coaching and other uses thinly disguised as academic. Graduates can use the money any way they choose.[51]

Since then 'til now the popular press has continued to have a field day on or around pageant time with pageant trivia; and the pageant still comes to you live and in color from Convention Hall some Saturday immediately after Labor Day on NBC. In 1989, the pageant crowned a third black queen, Debbye Turner, with little of the hoopla surrounding the first coronations.

Two changes in the format did occur: a) the contestants would once again be asked questions on stage (1988), and b) the new Miss America would be chosen, not from a group of six also-rans, but from she and the yet to be announced first runner-up (1988). Oddly, in 1990, *status quo* was restored by announcing the winner from a group of six, a decision that many media critics think unwise. This will be discussed in the next chapter.

Something else of note occurred in 1990. That year, Bert Parks patched things up with Miss America and returned for a cameo appearance. Some pageant insiders claim that the return was made possible by the death of Al Marks, the man who fired Parks. With a new person, Leonard Horn, presiding as Executive Director, old wounds could then be healed. Unfortunately, Bert's return would not be a happy one, at least not from an artistic point of view. His task was to announce the former Miss Americas in attendance. As he announced each name, the cameras would focus in on that particular Miss America. Half way through the presentation, Parks lost his place and announced the right name, but for the wrong person. Perplexed former winners grimaced in front of millions of home viewers as Parks continued the flawed roll call. This was an embarrassing comeback, indeed. For the record, those former Miss Americas in attendance were: Gretchen Carlson, Kaye Lani Raye Rafko, Kellye Cash, Susan Akin, Sharlene Wells, Debra Maffett, Susan Powell, Cheryl Prewitt, Kylene Barker, Susan Perkins, Dorothy Benham, Tawny Godin, Shirley Cothran, Laurel Schaefer, Phyllis George, Pamela Eldred, Judith Ford, Jane Jayroe, Deborah Bryant, Donna Axum, Maria Fletcher, Mary Ann Mobley, Marilyn Van Derbur, Lee Meriwether, Evelyn Ay, Yolande Betbeze, BeBe Shopp, Marilyn Meseke, and Marian Bergeron.

More embarrassed titters were evoked when Bert later rambled on about how the contestants should be called ladies. The 1990 pageant concluded with Parks singing "There She Is," a song which, like Burt, had made its comeback in 1985. This song was sung to the new Miss America, Marjorie Vincent, the fourth black winner. As the pageant concluded, host Gary Collins waved to the audiences and said, "See you next year."[52] He wouldn't. Ironically, Collins would hand in his resignation in early 1991. The new hosts would be TV personalities Regis Philbin and Kathy Lee Gifford.

Although this chronology of Miss America ends here, the history of the Miss America Pageant continues and will continue live from Atlantic City—a story to be told by future historians.

# Chapter X
# Finals: Last Words

It would be remiss to close this book without commenting on the effects of television on the pageant. Although pageant organizers and some authors emphasize that television has had no effect on the structure of the live pageant, data (much of it found in this book) conclude differently.[1] Television had, has and will leave its mark on the basic structure of the pageant as experienced live and in person in Convention Hall. These changes were not abrupt but rather gradual. That is, they did not happen "over night." One reason is that the *Miss America Pageant* was not a "made for television event." It was already an event for thirty three years prior to television coverage. This being the case, the event was not specifically structured, created, or tailored with television's biases in mind. The first televised pageant in 1954 was treated as a news event. That year, the television audience was supposed to be a non-intrusive guest of the proceedings. The cameras were merely to cover the action as it happened. The event, as such, was to proceed as usual without any changes or interference. However, this would not always be the case. Changes would occur slowly and almost invisibly.

One such change deals with the realm of time. The first televised *Miss America Pageant* in 1954 was telecast at 10:30 p.m. (EDT). Approximately one hundred and twenty five stations tuned in at that time. Others joined in at 11:00 p.m.[2] These stations covered a pageant already in progress. No special changes were made to accommodate the telecast. The live show for the Convention Hall audience remained as in years prior to television coverage at 8:30 p.m.

While the televised show's air time remained constant at 10:00 p.m., after television, the live show's start time for those at Convention Hall gradually changed. Each decade saw the actual start time of this live show "creep closer" to the 10:00 p.m. telecast time. By 1984, the live show and the televised show started at the same time, 10:00 p.m. Was this time slot determined with the West Coast affiliates in mind? The three hour time difference would place the last half (rather than the first half) of the pageant in prime time. An 8:30 p.m. telecast would air too early for prime time on the West Coast (5:30 p.m.) This might confirm that the 10:00 p.m. time slot was chosen with the West Coast affiliates in mind. However, this was not the case. The West Coast also aired the show, pre-taped, at 10:00 p.m. (PDT).[3] In 1984, the ratings in the West Coast were low. The winner had been announced by many news shows by air time. The low rating in the

West Coast, and the leak by the press, seem to indicate that the change in time was not in deference to the affiliates, and not because of potential ratings.

One might wonder why the show changed its time slot to 10:00 p.m. According to John Koushouris, the *Miss America Pageant* airs partially in prime time and partially out of prime time. This classifies the event as a Fringe Time, Class C event. Class C air time is at a cheaper rate than prime time air time.[4] Consequently, it can be assumed that the change in start time was due to the influence of television, though by television's economics not because of the affiliates or ratings. The live pageant changed its start time from 8:30 p.m. to 10:00 p.m. to concur with the television time, not the other way around.

Some would argue that television should have begun its coverage at the earlier hour, not because of any consideration to the Convention Hall audience, but because it made economic sense. Television shows, the *Miss America Pageant* included, depend on sponsors' fees for survival. Sponsors' fees are determined by ratings. More people can be reached during prime time. The change to 10:00 p.m. was made with frugality in mind, not television's biases. Perhaps this time slot is a remnant of earlier times when the insecurity of television's money-making potential was overshadowed by the pre-television mentality—start the live show at 8:30 p.m., get the gate receipts, and pay minimally for air rights. Today, any gate receipt would pale next to the television revenue. The original idea for the pageant to extend the Labor Day tourist season also is invalid today. Because of the casino industries, Atlantic City tourism is no longer dependent on good summer weather. Perhaps these temporal anachronisms will change in the near future.

One of the critics of the 10:00 p.m. Saturday night time slot is Frank Deford. He argues that if the pageant is to survive, it must make certain time changes. He recommends that the show should be aired the middle Saturday in August when people are really thinking about bathing beauties.[5]

Since the show is "family-oriented," it should begin at 7:30. This might insure a higher rating because younger audiences would still be able to watch. This earlier time slot would also be good for the network, since the *Miss America Pageant* could provide a lead-in audience. Deford claims that many curious viewers tuning in for the last few minutes of the pageant would keep the dial on that station and watch the following show.[6]

The idea to switch the time slot has been considered. Albert Marks, *Miss America Pageant* Executive Director, claims that the date of the pageant was switched from Saturday after Labor Day to the second Saturday in September for television. The day of the week and the time might also change in the near future. The reason is ratings.

This decision was made public by Marks in a press release to the national press in 1985. In New York, the story was covered by the *New York Post*. In an article lead by a banner statement, "TV Tradition to Become a Pawn in the Cutthroat Rating Game," Marks stated:

We're looking hard at a night other than Saturday night, and looking at going prime time on that night...we have [also] been approached about leaving [Atlantic City]. We have no interest in moving right now, but no one can predict the future.[7]

Al Marks was approached by this investigator after a press conference held during the 1986 *Miss America Pageant*. At the time, the investigator asked Marks the reason for the possible change in the time and day of the *Miss America Pageant*. He answered in one word: "Ratings." John Koushouris, *Miss America Pageant* producer, echoed this sentiment: "When making decisions, our main consideration is what will deliver the highest numbers—the lowest cost per the highest reach."[8]

The *Miss America Pageant* was originally created as a way to increase Atlantic City tourism and revenue. The *Miss America Pageant* was structured in such a way as to have many events held at different hours during different days, the reasoning being that to participate in these events, a person had to stay at the resort over an extended period of time. While at the resort, that person would spend money. The 1921 *Miss America Pageant* had a production allotment of $5,916. The city donated $1,000. This investment was to be recuperated with a profit margin of tourist dollars. By 1974, tourist dollars and Convention Hall gate receipts were incidental. The 1974 pageant had a budget of $127,000. The network (NBC-TV) and the sponsors combined paid $490,000 *for the final two hour telecast only*. By 1984, the sponsors and network were contributing $2,702,615 for the final telecast.[9] If the Boardwalk Parade and the three nights of Preliminaries were discontinued, and all that was left of the *Miss America Pageant* was the telecast of the Finals, the *Miss America Pageant* would still make money.

Under the above circumstances, it is remarkable that the pageant has not taken more of a "live audience be damned" attitude. That the Parade, the Preliminaries, and the pre-television show still exist shows some commitment to the live audience on the part of the *Miss America Pageant* hierarchy. Nevertheless, a change in start time would be in the best interest of everyone involved. The live audience would not have to be "baby sat" with a pre-television show. They would not have to wait until 10:00 p.m. either. The network might have a good lead-in for other shows. The sponsors might get a larger share of the market for the time slot. A new audience might be tapped. The sponsors would be able to raise the price for commercial spots. Because of new demographics, a new market might attract other sponsors. The contestants would reap the benefits both financially and via television exposure during prime time. If in the future the temporal accessibility of the pageant changes to prime time, it would be understandable, because it would be using television as befits its structure the best.

Another area in which the pageant was affected by television was in the area of public involvement and accessibility. In this instance, television coverage did not so much change the pageant as provide a perfect vehicle for justifying pageant attitudes concerning the relationship between those on stage and those not on stage. Media theorist Edmund Carpenter proposes that different media are better suited for the presentation of given ideas and insights.[10] As such, the pageant found a perfect host medium in television for the presentation of its ideas. This marriage of the pageant and television, at least as far as audience involvement is concerned, was a perfect and suitable union.

In way of explication, it is to be noted that the *Miss America Pageants* of the 1920s were created with audience participation in mind. Several gradual changes occurred in the history of the pageant, however, which assured that the interchange of information, audience input, and general information flow would be one way—from source to receiver; from stage to audience.

One circumstance propelling the *Miss America Pageant* closer to total uni-directional flow of information occurred in 1935. That year, with the change in management and presentational style, *viz.*, variety show, new rules and regulations were created. These rules, separating the contestants from the masses, erected the uni-directional barrier even further.

As the years progressed, new rules were created. Access to back stage areas was restricted. Contact with pageant personnel was monitored and checked by the use of a series of colored badges. Police and security officers guarded entrances and exits. Access to pageant activities other than the Parade were for ticket buyers only. Private functions were deemed off limits to everyone except those connected directly with the pageant.

Information about the contestants was also strictly controlled. Press releases were created and disseminated by a press committee. Press conferences were structured by that same committee. Contestants were chaperoned at all times. Information about the contestants, true or false, was disseminated a) through the press, b) through program information, c) through commentary by the master of ceremonies or television hosts, and d) through graphic information super-imposed over a video image. Contestant information was selectively disseminated, and received by the audience second-hand.

Changes in the judging system was another way that audience input was dissolved. In 1921, for example, winners were selected by fifty percent applause and fifty percent judges' choice. In 1922, audience input in the selection of a winner was replaced by judges' input only. This has remained constant from then until the present. Thousands of people prior to television and millions during television coverage have had no choice in the selection of Miss America. This might not seem an important issue unless one considers the social implications. Unlike team sports, but not unlike gymnastics, diving, shooting, skating and others where judges decide on form and performance, the outcome of the *Miss America Pageant* is subjective and arbitrary. A group of a few selected men and women determine which woman is the most beautiful, the most talented, the most deserving, the paragon of poise, the most all American, the "right image," and so forth any given year. Perhaps they are dictating, or perhaps the *Miss America Pageant* organizers, by choosing these judges, are dictating to the world that these judges' subjective tastes and predilections are what the world's should be. The subjective selection of ten semi-finalists by the few during the live preliminaries, dictate what the many will see on television. The judges, in effect, are gate-keepers in the information process; that is, they sift information, disseminating only select bits. The above speculation is an example of a subtle way in which television is uni-directional. It is an example of how in a uni-directional system, knowledge monopolies possess and disseminate information capriciously.[11] If the *Miss America Pageant* sources, through the judging system, are so doing, perhaps news sources, casting agencies, and other television programming not related to the *Miss America Pageant* are doing likewise.

Not only were the judges arbiters of taste and distributors of information, but so too were other sources. As the pageant expanded, new sources of information, *e.g.*, organizers, producers, choreographers, and the like, took the control from the audience's hands. In the early pageants, the form of the events dictated audience participation. The dances and the balls were molded, for better or for worse, by the participants. The Rolling Chair Parade, the Bathers' Revue, and the costume parties were created for, and consequently had, audience participation. As the *Miss America Pageant* became more and more organized: more and more "sources" had control over more and more specialized domains, *e.g.*, the press, the tickets, the music, and so forth. Slowly but surely, the audience became completely passive—guided to see what was meant to be seen; hear what was meant to be heard; reacting when and how they were meant to react. Pageant organizers argue that the pageant is more than just one week in September. It is a fifty-two week a year endeavor with participation at all levels. Perhaps, but to the majority of Americans, the pageant is still that which occurs that Saturday in September. As such, pageant involvement of even the most minimal kind is non-existent to the masses.

As alluded to above, part of the decline in audience input had to do with changes in the form of the events. When the *Miss America Pageant* became a theatrical variety show in 1935, the audience was not expected to participate or provide input. Physically, a theatrical event is structured so that the audience in the house sits passively in the dark and is entertained, informed, amused, and so on by those on the lit stage. This situation was perfect for television.

Changes in the physical form of the pageant also changed the structure of the pageant. As demonstrated above, with the advent of television, much of the commentary was directed to the television audience by a television color commentator. Again, this changed when a change in form occurred— the introduction of the Convention Hall giant video screens. The information for the television audience and the information for the live audience became one. Blurring even more this line between the home and the Convention Hall audience was that the program booklet, a tool previously endemic to the live audience, could be pre-purchased by stay-at-homes. Information once solely for those attending live and in person was now available for stay-at-homes. Stay-at-homes could also stay abreast of pageant events by tuning in to television entertainment or news shows, reading magazines, and daily newspapers—all full of pageant "tidbits." Conversely, live audiences could become home audiences and see the pageant from a different perspective, in a different communication environment, via the technology of video taping. After the advent of television coverage, the line between live and televised, here and there, now and later became fuzzy. As the form of the pageant changed, so did the relationship between the audience and the pageant. This seems to confirm Harold A. Innis' assumption that "a medium of communication has an important influence on the dissemination of knowledge over time and space."[12] To paraphrase Marshall McLuhan, time ceased, space vanished, and the *Miss America Pageant* became a simultaneous happening. The *Miss America Pageant* strongly proved the power of television to invest an occasion with the character of corporate participation.[13]

Not only such intangibles as time and involvement have been affected by television, but also such concrete aspects as form and shape. The *Miss America Pageant* has always been a visual event. A beauty pageant by its name implies that physical, visual beauty would be on display. The costuming, the production numbers, the scenery, and the blocking within a theatrical setting, *i.e.*, stage and house, made the pageant visual. Because television is predominantly a visual medium, the transition to television was smooth, especially considering that television coverage for the first pageant was nonintrusive. The cameras just picked up the action "as is."

As time progressed, television became intrusive. Changes in the visual form started occurring. The most obvious of those changes was the added and cumulative use of choreography and movement. Static moments were eliminated. The elimination of such traditional trappings as the robe, flowers, and sash in 1974 was not so much an attempt at modernization than an attempt to speed up the proceedings. The coronation lasted one minute in 1964, forty seconds in 1974, and fifteen seconds in 1984. In 1988, host Gary Collins, half-jokingly admonished the abdicating Miss America to speed up the crowning of her successor. To assure that the finals run smoothly, the Preliminaries serve as dress rehearsals for the Saturday night telecast.[14]

Changes in the visuals influenced by television coverage also included the use and avoidance of white and certain colors during the early color casts. The change in sets from box sets to open sets were also influenced by television. The newer sets afforded more visual variety. A cyclorama changed a mere wall into a moonlit night. Scenery could be flown in or out right in front of the audience's eyes. This not only sped up the scene changes, but added movement. Visually, the open sets also allowed the cameras to "shoot" from different angles.

The blocking also changed during the time of television. Most of the blocking done prior to television coverage was to the audience. With television, the blocking was to the camera. Many times, the live audience was completely ignored. Commercials were introduced to the camera. Dancers mugged and posed for the camera. Because of the large cast size, the constant motion, and dialogue or motion directed to the cameras set in different areas of the Hall, a person sitting there could easily lose track of who was saying or doing what. This was remedied by the introduction of the giant screens. All televised action was shown to the live audience. The audience could see close-ups and reactions, flash backs, and graphic information, as well as video images of past events. The live audience could even see themselves watching themselves watching themselves (*ad infinitum*).

Perhaps one change that most media analysts would agree should occur in the pageant is the final moment when Miss America is crowned.[15] Because it is a contest, the *Miss America Pageant* is dramatically and sequentially structured. Because television is biased towards this dramatic, sequential structure, the transition to television was fluid. In 1972, however, the final moment of the competition, and therefore, the drama, was changed. Perhaps seeing no need for five finalists after the on-stage interviews were eliminated, Miss America was chosen from a line of ten. The *Miss America Pageant* organizers said that this adds to the drama because you have six women left.[16] Some might argue that this is a lame excuse since all the strong contenders have been already named as runners-up at that point. This change, rather than adding to the drama, turned the moment into a denouement. It was anti-climactic. In Frank Deford's words:

In any competition, the ultimate is the faceoff: one on one. Nothing was tenser at Miss America than the minute the two survivors sat side by side one about to be named first runner-up, to live forever in oblivion, the other to have a year of being Miss America. But for the past few years, the top runners-up have been announced and removed from the scene, leaving the new queen amidst five also-rans. At what should be the climax, the air goes out of the whole balloon.[17]

However, for some unknown reason, in 1988, the coronation format was changed. The two candidates with the most votes were called forward after the fourth, third, and second runner-ups had been named. This was the build-up of high drama: the two possible Miss Americas clenched hands; the cameras closed in on the hyper-ventilating twosome; the audience suspended breathing for the moment; the announcement of the first runner-up. The new Miss America was left sobbing for all to see. There was high drama, indeed. However, much to the chagrin of many, in 1990, the winner was once again chosen out of the pack. Who knows if this will change again in the future. For that matter, who can predict what other changes the pageant will undergo in future years?

Meanwhile, it is important to continue to study this and other similar events such as the *Academy Awards*, the *World Series*, and the *Macy's Thanksgiving Day Parade*, because much can be learned about ourselves by studying the social importance, significance, and relevance of events coming live from Atlantic City, Hollywood, or the world.

# Notes

*Foreword*

[1]"Won By a Nose," *New York Daily News* 15 Sept. 1982: 2; Brendan Gill, "The Miss America Uproar: What it Says About Us All," *TV Guide* 15-21 Sept. 1984; "Vanessa the Undressa Loses Crown," *New York Post* 21 July 1984: 1; Peggy Moran, "Here She Comes, Broke," *Atlantic City Magazine* Sept. 1987: 49; Roger Capetini, "Miss America Stole My Husband," *National Enquirer* 12 Feb. 1991: 51; Kate Caldwell, "There She Grows...Miss America Packs on Hefty 20 Lbs.," *Star* 12 Feb. 1991: 6.

[2]Lois Banner, *American Beauty* (New York: Knopf, 1983).

[3]Charles E. Funnel, *By the Beautiful Sea: The Rise and High Times of that Great Resort, Atlantic City* (Rutgers: Rutgers UP, 1983); William McMahon, *So Young...So Gay* (Atlantic City: Atlantic City P, 1970); Vicki Gold Levi and Lee Eisenberg, *Atlantic City: 125 Years of Ocean Madness* (New York: Clarkson N. Potter, 1979).

[4]Frank Deford, *There She Is: The Life and Times of Miss America* (1971; New York: Viking, 1978).

[5]Nancie Martin, *Miss America Through the Looking Glass: The Story Behind the Scenes* (New York: Simon and Schuster, 1985).

[6]Marjorie Ford, *Sharing the Crown* (Litchfield, IL: Publications Investments, 1971).

[7]William Goldman, *Hype and Glory* (New York: Villard, 1991).

[8]Jacques Mercer, *How to Win a Beauty Contest* (Phoenix, AZ: Curran, 1960); Cheryl Prewitt with Kathryn Stalby, *A Bright Shining Place: The Story of a Miracle* (New York: Doubleday, 1981); Susan Dworkin, *Miss America 1945: Bess Myerson's Own Story* (New York: New Market P, 1987).

[9]Henry Pang, "Miss America: an American Ideal," *Journal of Popular Culture* (Spring 1969): 695.

[10]Ross Milloy, "Almost Miss America," *TV Guide*, 4-10 Sept. 1982.

[11]Abigail Rockmore, Producer; John Stoessel, Correspondent, "The Youngest Beauty Queens," *20/20* ABC News Transcript (New York: Journal Graphics): July 25, 1985.

[12]Geoffrey Dunn and Mark Schwartz, Directors; Dunn, Schwartz and Claire Rubach, Producers; ed. Schwartz, *Miss...or Myth?* (Distributors: Cinema Guild, 1987).

[13]Dunn and Schwartz; A.R. Riverol published an article titled "Miss America and Other Misses: A Second Look at the American Beauty Contests," *Etc.* (Summer 1983): 207-217. The documentary cited above, although having a similar title, focuses on different aspects of beauty contests.

[14]Neil Postman, *Teaching as a Conserving Activity* (New York: Dell, 1979): 196.

[15]Further analysis of the impact of television on the *Miss America Pageant* can be found in Riverol, A., *The Miss America Pageant; A Comparative Structural Analysis of the Pre- and Post-Television Event* (New York University, 1988), the doctoral dissertation upon which much of this book is based.

### Chapter I

[1]Much of the material presented in this chapter is based on an article written by the author while developing this book. This article appeared in *Etc.*, (Summer 1983) under the title "Myth America and Other Misses: A Second Look at the American Beauty Contests."

[2]Lois Banner, *American Beauty* (New York: Knopf, 1983) 249.

[3]Brownmiller cites the speech made by an unidentified protester at the 1968 *Miss America Pageant* in Susan Brownmiller, *Femininity* (New York: Linden, 1984) 24-25.

[4]Banner 250.

[5]Banner 250.

[6]Banner 251.

[7]Banner 251.

[8]For details on how belles were selected in nineteenth century America, see Banner, 104.

[9]Banner 255.

[10]Banner 256.

[11]Siegfried Giedion, *Mechanization Takes Command* (1947; New York: Norton, 1975) 651-53.

[12]Giedion 652-53, 659.

[13]Charles Panati, *Extraordinary Origins of Everyday Things* (New York: Harper and Row, 1987) 321.

[14]Giedion 660-61.

[15]Panati 321.

[16]Panati 321.

[17]Panati 321.

[18]Banner 80.

[19]Frank Deford, *There She Is: The Life and Times of Miss America* (1971; New York: Viking, 1978).

[20]Deford.

[21]Banner 267.

[22]Panati 321.

[23]Panati 322.

### Chapter II

[1]Louis St. John, "In the Twenties," *1960 Miss America Pageant Yearbook* [program]: np. St. John was on the original committee.

[2]Frank Deford, *There She Is: The Life and Times of Miss America* (1971; New York: Viking, 1978).

[3]St. John.

[4]Herb Test, "Bathers' Revue Unique Among Pageant Fetes," *Atlantic City Daily Press* (ACDP), 7 Sept. 1921: 1; "Neptune Arrives, Waves Magic Trident, and Super Carnival Grips Resort," ACDP, 8 Sept. 1921.

[5]"Neptune Arrives."

[6]"King Neptune Opens Seashore Pageant," *New York Times* (NYT), 7 Sept. 1922: 26; also "Hudson Maxim to be Father Neptune," ACDP, 5 Sept. 1921; St. John.

[7]"Neptune Arrives."

[8]Various reports, ACDP, September 5-11, 1921; "Neptune Arrives"; Deford 117.

[9]"Pageant Program," ACDP, 7 Sept. 1921: 1.

[10]"Neptune Arrives."

[11]"Neptune Arrives."

[12]Victor Jagmetty, "Beach Combers," ACDP, 7 Sept. 1921: 9.

[13]"Neptune Arrives."

[14]Jagmetty 9.

[15]"Pageant Program."

[16]Atlantic Foto Service, untitled (data from caption under photograph), ACDP, 8 Sept. 1921: 1.

[17]"Pageant Program"; "Neptune Arrives."

[18]"Neptune Arrives"; "Curtain Rolls Back on Big Pageant—Beauties Captivate Great Throngs," ACDP, 7 Sept. 1921: 7.

[19]"Neptune Arrives."

[20]"Neptune Arrives."

[21]"Night Carnival Draws Great Crowd to 'Walk,' " ACDP, 8 Sept. 1921: 1; "Pageant Program."

[22]"Pageant Program."

[23]"Night Carnival" 1, 5.

[24]"Pageant Program" 1; "Night Carnival" 1, 5.

[25]"Night Carnival" 5.

[26]"Night Carnival" 5.

[27]Vicki Gold Levi and Lee Eisenberg, *Atlantic City: 125 Years of Ocean Madness* (New York: Clarkson N. Potter, 1979) 188-90.

[28]"Night Carnival" 5.

[29]"Night Carnival" 5.

[30]Deford 113.

[31]Advertisements appeared in the ACDP throughout the week beginning September 5, 1921.

[32]"Why Not Enter the Bathers' Revue?" ACDP, 5 Sept. 1921: 9.

[33]"Bathers' Revue."

[34]"Pageant Program" 1; "Gorgeous Beauty Feature of Climaxing Spectacles in City's Great Pageant," ACDP, 9 Sept. 1921: 1; "Bathers' Revue," ACDP, 9 Sept. 1921: 1; "Gorgeous Beauty Feature" 1.

[35]"Gorgeous Beauty Feature" 1.

[36]Deford 113.

[37]Deford.

[38]Deford.

[39]Deford 12.

[40]"Press Scoops," ACDP, 9 Sept. 1921: 1.

[41]"Gorgeous Beauty Feature" 12.

[42]"Gorgeous Beauty Feature."

[43]"Gorgeous Beauty Feature" 1.

[44]For contemporary rolling chairs, this information has been gathered by the author from personal observation.

[45]Levi and Eisenberg 45-52.

[46]"Pageant Program"; "Gorgeous Beauty Feature."

[47]"The Chair Parade," ACDP, 9 Sept. 1921: 1.

[48]"Pageant Program."

[49]"Pageant Program."

[50]"Miss Washington Carries Away Golden Mermaid," ACDP, 9 Sept. 1921: 12.

[51]"Complete Prize List," ACDP, 9 Sept. 1921: 1.

[52]"Miss Washington Wins."

[53]"Miss Washington Wins" 12; "Grand Prize Award in Division No. 6," ACDP, 5 Sept. 1921 (Boardwalk Edition): 1.

[54]"Miss Washington Wins" 12.

[55]"Pageant in Wide Favor With Many Urging Longer Duration of the Frolic," ACDP, 10 Sept. 1921: 1.

[56]"Pageant."

[57]"Pageant Film Popular," ACDP, 10 Sept. 1921: 1.

[58]"Miss America Started in 1921 as Falc"; Deford 115; "Beauty Fete Ready at Atlantic City," *New York Times* (NYT), 6 Sept. 1922: 10.

[59]Edward P. Beach, "Epidemic of Beauty About to Hit Town," ACDP, 4 Sept. 1922: 1; Edward P. Beach, "Resort Fairly Bulges Beauty for Big Fete," ACDP, 5 Sept. 1923: 1; "Pageant at Atlantic City," NYT, 1 Sept. 1924: 24; "Today's Pageant Program," ACDP, 8 Sept. 1922: 1.

[60]"Miss Indianapolis is Prettiest Girl," NYT, 8 Sept. 1922: 20; "Miss Manhattan Scores," NYT, 5 Sept. 1924: 6; St. John; Deford 131.

[61]Charles E. Funnell, *By the Beautiful Sea: The Rise and High Times of That Great American Resort, Atlantic City* (1975; New Brunswick, NJ: Rutgers UP, 1983) 148.

[62]"Crowd Goes Wild Over Marvelous Spectacle Two Miles in Length," ACDP, 8 Sept. 1922: 1. This citation described the Rolling Chair Parade.

[63]Deford 115; "Neptune Arrives"; "Beauty Fete" 10; "Scores of Beauties Headed for Pageant," NYT, 5 Sept. 1922; "Fall Carnival Holds Sway in Atlantic City," NYT, 6 Sept. 1923: 28; "Beauties Arrive at Shore Pageant," NYT, 2 Sept. 1924.

[64]"Neptune Arrives" 1; "Girl Makes Dash from Alaska to Enter Pageant Tournament," ACDP, 2 Sept. 1922: 1; Deford 131.

[65]"Three-Ply Holiday Gives Resort Mighty Guest List," ACDP, 4 Sept. 1922: 1; Deford 115.

[66]"Girl Makes Dash"; "Bewildering Display of Beauty Gives Great Multitude a Thrill Along 'Walk," ACDP, 7 Sept. 1923: 1; "Miss Manhattan Scores."

[67]Deford 111.

[68]Letter from Adrian Phillips, Absecon, New Jersey, August 7, 1987.

[69]Letter from Lenora S. Slaughter Frappart, Scottsdale, Arizona, August 7, 1987.

[70]"Atlantic City to Drop Its Outdoor Pageant," NYT, 12 Mar. 1928: 13; St. John; Deford 129.

[71]"Attacks Bathing Review," NYT, 11 Sept. 1923: 15; "Criticism Well Deserved," NYT, April, 1924: 16; "Some Behind-Time Knocking," ACDP, 1 Sept. 1925: 13; "Attack Beauty Pageant," NYT, 1 Mar. 1927: 3; "Women Open Fight on Beauty Pageant," NYT, 18 Nov. 1927: 12; "Bishop Condemns Beauty Pageant," NYT, 30 Nov. 1927: 10.

[72]See Daniel Boorstin, *The Image* (1961; New York: Antheum, 1980) 10-11.

#### Chapter III

[1]Letter from Marian Bergeron, Kettering, Ohio, August 11, 1987.

[2]"30 Beauties Open Pageant for '33 Title," *Atlantic City Daily Press* (ACDP), 6 Sept. 1933: 1.

[3]"30 Beauties" 9.

[4]See Daniel J. Boorstin, *The Image* (1961; New York: Antheum, 1980) 10-11.

[5]"30 Beauties."

[6]"30 Beauties" 9.

[7]"30 Beauties" 9.

[8]"30 Beauties" 9.

[9]"Today's Pageant Program," ACDP, 7 Sept. 1933: 1.

[10]"Pageant Beauty Ball Colorful Fete; Natty Morris Guards Act as Escorts," ACDP, 7 Sept. 1933: 12.

[11]"Today's Program."

[12]"Pageant Beauty Ball" 9.

[13]"Pageant Beauty Ball" 9.

[14]"Miss New York Wins Gold Cup for Pageant Girls," ACDP, 8 Sept. 1933: 1; "Today's Program."

[15]"Pageant Beauty Ball" 12.

[16]"Miss New York Wins" 18.

[17]"Today's Program."

[18]"Miss New York Wins" 18.

[19]"Miss New York Wins" 18.

[20]"Miss New York Wins" 1.

[21]"Miss New York Wins" 18.

[22]"Miss New York Wins" 1.

[23]"Miss New York Wins" 1.

[24]"Beauty Title Lines Field Against N.Y.," ACDP, 9 Sept. 1933: 12.

[25]"Beauty Title."

[26]See the previous Chapter.

[27]"Beauty Title Lines Field Against N.Y."

[28]"Beauty Title."

[29]"Today's Pageant Events," ACDP, 9 Sept. 1933: 1.

[30]"Stage, Screen Offers Made Miss America," ACDP, 11 Sept. 1933.

[31]"Stage, Screen Offers."

[32]"Stage, Screen Offers."

[33]Frank Deford, *There She Is: The Life and Times of Miss America* (1971; New York: Viking, 1978) 136.

[34]"Stage, Screen Offers"; Deford 136; Letter from Marian Bergeron.

[35]Letter from Marian Bergeron.

[36]"Stage, Screen Offers" 1, 4; Louis St. John, "In the Twenties," *The 1960 Miss America Pageant Yearbook* [program]: 1.

[37]"Beauty Queen Chosen," NYT, 5 Oct. 1934: 7; Helena Mack was chosen second runner-up in the 1943 MAP as Miss Boston. It is not known if this is the same person as the American Queen of Beauty.

[38]Louis St. John, "In 1935," *The 1960 Miss America Pageant Yearbook* [program]: 9.

[39]Louis St. John. "Boardwalk Spectacle Will Be Staged Tomorrow if Weather Permits," *Atlantic City Press* (ACP), 6 Sept. 1935: 1; "Miss Pittsburgh Wins Beauty Crown," NYT, 8 Sept. 1935: 25.

[40]St. John, "In 1935."

[41]St. John. Deford 150; Susan Dworkin, *Miss America, 1945: Bess Myerson's Own Story* (New York: New Market, 1987) 95-96.

[42]Dworkin 95-96.

[43]"Boardwalk Spectacle"; "Miss Pittsburgh Wins Beauty Crown."

[44]"Miss Pittsburgh Wins Beauty Crown."

[45]"Miss California Wins," NYT, 4 Sept. 1935: 22.

[46]"Bronx Girl Chosen in Bathing-Suit Event in Atlantic City," NYT, 5 Sept. 1935: 25.

[47]St. John, "In 1935"; "Today's Jubilee Program," ACP, 6 Sept. 1935: 1; "Boardwalk Spectacle" 18.

[48]"The Silver Anniversary of the Miss Americas," *1951 Miss America Pageant Yearbook* [program], no pagination.

[49]"Miss America Standards Have Changed Throughout the Years," ACP, 7 Sept. 1954: 6.

[50]St. John, "In 1935"; "Miss Pittsburgh Wins Beauty Crown."

[51]St. John, "In 1935."

[52]Deford 150.

[53]Louis St. John, "In 1936," *1960 Miss America Pageant Yearbook* [program]: 11; Deford 150; Dworkin 96.

[54]St. John, "In 1936."

[55]St. John, "In 1936"; Louis St. John, "1937 History," *1960 Miss America Pageant Yearbook* [program]: 13.

[56]St. John, "In 1937."

[57]St. John.

[58]St. John. "In 1937"; Deford 140-46.

[59]Louis St. John, "In 1938," *1960 Miss America Pageant Yearbook* 15.

[60]Louis St. John, "In 1939," *1960 Miss America Pageant Yearbook* 17; Deford 330.

[61]St. John, "In 1938"; Deford 152; Dworkin 96.

*Chapter IV*

[1]"Miss America Standards Have Changed Throughout the Years"; Susan Dworkin, *Miss America 1945: Bess Myerson's Own Story* (New York: New Market, 1987) 97.

[2]"Miss America Standards."

[3]"Miss America Standards"; Dworkin 97; Frank Deford, *There She Is: The Life and Times of Miss America* (1971; New York: Viking, 1978) 153.

[4]Deford 153; "Miss America Standards."

[5]Louis St. John, "In 1941," *1960 Miss America Pageant Year Book* [program]: 21; This rule went into effect after Rosaemary La Planche, first runner-up in 1940, became MA 1941.

[6]Louis St. John.

[7]Deford 153.

[8]Dworkin 97.

[9]Dworkin.

[10]Louis St. John, "In 1943," *1960 Miss America Pageant Yearbook* [program]: 25.

[11]Louis St. John.

[12]In Dworkin, 97-98; Amount of payment is cited in St. John, "In 1943."

[13]"Pageant Beauties Arrive in Phila[delphia] Today, Due Here Tuesday Noon," ACP, 6 Sept. 1943: 1, 8.

[14]St. John, "In 1943."

[15]Advertisement for tickets, ACP, 5 Sept. 1943: 6; "Pageant Beauties Arrive In Phila[delphia]."

[16]St. John, "In 1943"; "Pageant Beauties" 8.

[17]"Miss America Beauty, Health, and Talent Pageant," NYT, 5 Sept. 1943: 10.

[18]St. John, "In 1943"; "'American Beauty Special' to Bring 33 Pageant Girls," ACP, 7 Sept. 1943: 1.

[19]"Pageant Beauties" 8.

[20]"Miss California First To Score," ACP, 9 Sept. 1943: 10.

[21]"Miss California." Picture in "In 1943" depicts runway set-up.

[22]"Miss California."

[23]Ollie Crawford, "Miss California is Again Winner," ACP, 11 Sept. 1943: 1.

[24]"Miss California First to Score" 10; "Miss Boston Triumphs Again," ACP, 10 Sept. 1943: 22.

[25]"Miss California First"; Ollie Crawford, "Blonde Jean Bartel New Beauty Queen," ACP, 12 Sept. 1943: 1.

[26]Various reports, ACP, 8-10 Sept. 1943.

[27]"Pageant Ice Skater Without Ice Piles Up Trouble for Backers," ACP, 11 Sept. 1943: 10.

[28]"Pageant".

[29]"Miss California First to Score"; "Miss Boston Triumphs Again" 1; Crawford, "Miss California" 1; "American Beauty Special" 8; Various reports, ACP, September 8-10.

[30]Crawford, "Blonde Jean Bartel."

[31]Crawford.

[32]Crawford.

[33]Crawford, "Blonde Jean Bartel."

[34]Crawford.

[35]Crawford.

[36]Crawford, "Blonde Jean Bartel."

[37]St. John, "In 1943"; Dworkin 98; Lenora Slaughter claims that 100 cities were visited; Deford claims that 34 cities were visited and that $250,000,000 in Series E Bonds were sold by Bartel (157). Deford does not cite his source of information.

[38]Reports in St. John "In 1943," Dworkin 98, and Deford 159, credit Bartel, Slaughter or sorority women at Kappa Kappa Gamma with the idea.

[39]Dworkin 99.

[40]Letter from Lenora Slaughter Frapart.

[41]Dworkin 1987.

[42]According to Deford, E. B. Stewart, President of sponsor Catalina Swimsuits, insisted that people bathed in a tub and swam in a swimsuit (64); Louis St. John, "In 1947," 1960 Miss America Pageant Yearbook 33; Louis St. John, "In 1948," 1960 Miss America Pageant Yearbook 34; Although MA 1933 was crowned in evening gown, it was in 1948 that the official "policy" took effect; Louis St. John, "In 1949," 1960 Miss America Pageant Yearbook 35.

### Chapter V

[1]Frank Deford, There She Is: The Life and Times of Miss America. (1971; New York: Viking, 1978) 180.

[2]Deford 175.

[3]Louis St. John, "In 1950," 1960 Miss America Yearbook 39.

[4]Louis St. John.

[5]Various reports in ACP and NYT, 8 Sept. 1953 through 13 Sept. 1953; Sam Schor, "Famous Miss America Pageant, Miss Slaughter Masterminds," ACP, 8 Sept. 1953: 11.

[6]"Foreword," 1953 Souvenir Book of the Miss America Pageant 1.

[7]Louis St. John, "In 1953," 1960 Miss America Pageant Yearbook [program] 45; Sam Schor, "Famous Miss America Pageant"; Harmon Nichols, "Boardwalk No-Man's Land As Pageant Girls Arrive," ACP, 8 Sept. 1953: 11.

[8]Carlo Sardella, "Eddie Fisher Heads March Throngs Hail Arriving Girls," ACP, 8 Sept. 1953: 1.

[9]Carlo Sardella, "Boardwalk Jammed," ACP, 9 Sept. 1953: 1.

[10]"Lineup for Today's Pageant Parade," ACP, 8 Sept. 1953: 11.

[11]Sardella, "Boardwalk Jammed" 10.

[12]Ibid.; Personal Interview with Miss America 1954, Evelyn Ay, 13 Sept. 1986; "Pageant Parade Winners," ACP, 9 Sept. 1953: 1.

¹³Various reports, ACP, 8-13 Sept. 1953; "Today's Pageant Program," ACP, 11 Sept. 1953: 3; Schor, "Famous Miss America Pageant"; Carlo Sardella, "Pageant Thrills Film Star Judge," ACP, 11 Sept. 1953: 1.

¹⁴"1953 Miss America Pageant Program of Events," *1953 Miss America Souvenir Book* 24-25; St. John, "In 1953."

¹⁵"May Reported Ill; Owen Pageant Emcee," ACP 11 Sept. 1953: 1; Carlo Sardella, "Resort Ripples," ACP, 14 Sept. 1953: 11.

¹⁶"Miss America Pageant Program of Events"; "Pageant Sidelights," ACP, 10 Sept. 1953: 1, 12.

¹⁷Among the fifty contestants were representatives from Puerto Rico and Canada.

¹⁸"1953 Miss America Pageant Program of Events."

¹⁹"1953 Miss America Pageant Program."

²⁰"Pageant Sidelights" 12.

²¹"1953 MAP Program"; "Pageant Sidelights," 10 Sept. 1953: 12.

²²"1953 MAP Program."

²³Carlo Sardella, "5,800 Watch As Pennsylvania Wins in Swimming Suit and Virginia in Talent Competition," ACP, 12 Sept. 1953: 1, 12; Harmon W. Nichols, "Beauty Sets School Talk," ACP, 10 Sept. 1953: 1, 12; "1953 MAP Program."

²⁴"Pageant Sidelights," 10 Sept. 1953: 12.

²⁵"5,800 Watch As Pennsylvania Wins in Swimming Suit And Virginia in Talent Competition," *Atlantic City Press* 10 Sept. 1953: 1, 12; "S. Dakota, Wyoming Win Honors," 11 Sept. 1953: 1; Carlo Sardella, "Delaware Wins in Talent," 12 Sept. 1953: 1.

²⁶Sardella, "Miss Pennsylvania" 1, 7.

²⁷Interview with Evelyn Ay; "1953 MAP Program."

²⁸Sardella, "Miss Pennsylvania" 7.

²⁹Sardella, "Miss Pennsylvania" 7; "1953 MAP Program."

³⁰"1953 MAP Program"; Sardella, "Miss Pennsylvania" 7.

³¹"1953 MAP Program"; Sardella, "Miss Pennsylvania," 7.

³²"1953 MAP Program"; Sardella, "Miss Pennsylvania," 1, 7.

³³"1953 MAP Program"; Sardella, "Miss Pennsylvania" 1.

³⁴Sardella, "Miss Pennsylvania" 1, 7.

³⁵Interview with Evelyn Ay.

### Chapter VI

¹Louis St. John, "In 1954," *1960 Miss America Pageant Yearbook* [program] 47.

²St. John, "In 1953," 45.

³St. John, "In 1954."

⁴"In 1954"; "125 Stations to Carry Live Pageant Telecast," ACP, 7 Sept. 1954: 1.

⁵"In 1954"; "125 Stations."

⁶"In 1954"; "Program of Final Contest," *1954 Miss America Pageant* [program] 27; "125 Stations."

⁷Interview with John Koushouris, MAP Producer, 15 May 1987; Interview with Evelyn Ay Sempier; Letter from Lee Meriwether, c/o MAP, 11 August 1987.

⁸"125 Stations."

⁹"In 1954"; Jim Tomlinson, "Innovations to Put Zip Into Pageant," ACP, 5 Sept. 1954: 1.

¹⁰Tomlinson 1.

¹¹"In 1954."

¹²"Walk Parade Will Start at 8:30 P.M.," ACP, 7 Sept. 1954: 1; Ralph Villers, "200,000 Persons Watch Beauties," ACP, 8 Sept. 1954: 1, 28; "In 1954."

[13]Villers 28.

[14]Sam Schor, "Pageant Parade Sidelights," ACP, 8 Sept. 1954: 1.

[15]Villers 1; "In 1954."

[16]Villers 1; "In 1954."

[17]Schor 1.

[18]Villers 1.

[19]Villers 1; John L. Boucher, "6,000 Attend First Night of Preliminary Judging," ACP, 9 Sept. 1954: 1.

[20]"Program of Preliminary Contests," *1954 Miss America Pageant* [program] 24-25.

[21]Entertainment provided between competitive events was called "divertissement" in the "Program of Preliminary Contests," 24-25.

[22]Among the fifty contestants were representatives from Puerto Rico and Canada.

[23]John L. Boucher, "6,100 View Final Preliminary," ACP, 11 Sept. 1954: 1.

[24]Boucher, "6,000 Attend"; John L. Boucher, "Miss Florida Wins Swim Suit Event," ACP, 10 Sept. 1954.

[25]"Program of Preliminary Contests"; Boucher, "Miss Florida Wins."

[26]Boucher, "6,000 Attend" 10; Tomlinson 1; "Program of Preliminary Contests."

[27]Boucher.

[28]"Program of Preliminary Contests."

[29]Various reports, ACP, 8-10 Sept. 1954.

[30]"Program of Preliminary Contests."

[31]Various reports, ACP, 8-10 Sept. 1954.

[32]Boucher, "6,000 Attend" 10; Boucher, "6,000 Attend" 1; Boucher, "Miss Florida Wins" 1; Boucher, "6,100 View" 1.

[33]John L. Boucher, "Miss Florida First Runner-Up," ACP, 12 Sept. 1954: 1, 18.

[34]"Program of Final Contest," *1954 Miss America Pageant* [program] 27.

[35]Boucher, "Miss Florida 1st Runner-Up" 18; "Miss Congeniality," ACP, 12 Sept. 1954: 18.

[36]"In 1954"; Letter from Lee Meriwether; "Program of Final Contest"; Boucher, "Miss Florida First Runner-Up" 18.

[37]Letter from Lee Meriwether; Boucher, "Miss Florida 1st Runner-Up" 18.

[38]"In 1954"; Boucher, "Miss Florida 1st Runner-Up" 18.

[39]Letter from Lee Meriwether.

[40]Boucher, "Miss Florida 1st Runner-Up" 1.

[41]Frank Deford, *There She Is: The Life and Times of Miss America* (1971; New York: Penguin, 1978) 204.

[42]Boucher, "Miss Florida 1st Runner-Up"; "Program of Final Contest"; Letter from Lee Meriwether.

[43]John L. Boucher, "Miss America Whispered Words to Dead Father at Coronation," ACP, 13 Sept. 1954: 1, 16; Letter from Lee Meriwether; Deford 193; *Miss America Pageant National Show Statistics*, Unpublished documents provided by MAP offices; Statistics obtained directly from A. C. Nielsen.

[44]When a change mentioned in one year is not mentioned the following year, it can be assumed that it remained the same; Louis St. John, "In 1955," *The 1960 Miss America Pageant Yearbook* [program] 49; "1956," *Miss America Pageant Show Statistics 1951-[1985]*, unpublished document provided by the MAP offices; Louis St. John, "In 1957," *The 1957 Miss America Pageant Yearbook* [program] 52; "1957," *Miss America Pageant Show Statistics 1951-[1985]*, unpublished document provided by the MAP offices; Louis St. John, "In 1958," *The 1960 Miss America Pageant Yearbook* [program] 57; Video tape of the

1958 pageant; Louis St. John, "In 1959," *The 1960 Miss America Pageant Yearbook* [program] 59.

*Chapter VII*

[1]"1960," *Miss America Pageant Show Statistics 1951-[1985]*, unpublished document provided by the MAP offices.

[2]Letter from Lee Meriwether; Letter from Vonda Kay Van Dyke Scoates, 31 August 1987.

[3]"1963," *Show Statistics*.

[4]"1962," *Miss America Pageant Show Statistics 1951-[1985]*, unpublished document provided by the MAP offices.

[5]"1961," *Show Statistics*.

[6]"1962"; "1963," *Show Statistics*.

[7]Interview with John Koushouris.

[8]Advertisement, ACP, 8 Sept. 1964; Frank J. Prendergast, "150,000 See Colorful Pageant Parade," ACP, 9 Sept. 1964: 1.

[9]Frank J. Prendergast, "150,000."

[10]Prendergast 19.

[11]See *A 40 Year Report of the Miss America Scholarship Pageant Scholarship Foundation 1945-1985*, booklet provided by the Miss America Pageant Office; See Mark Hessler, "Miss Atlantic City Greeter 'Humiliated,' Quits Post," ACP, 10 Sept. 1964: 21.

[12]Mark Hessler, "Miss Atlantic City Greeter 'Humiliated', Quits Post."

[13]"Parade Winners," ACP, 9 Sept. 1964: 1.

[14]"Here's How Pageant Picks Miss America," ACP, 10 Sept. 1964: 7.

[15]Frank J. Prendergast, "N. Dakotan, W. Virginian Win in Talent, Swim Suit," ACP, 11 Sept. 1964: 14.

[16]"Here's How Pageant Picks [MA]."

[17]"Program of Preliminary Competitions," *1964 Miss America Pageant* [Program] 31.

[18]According to "Program of Preliminary Competitions," red, blue, and gold were colors found in New Jersey's State Seal. The theme of the 1964 MAP was "Happy Birthday, Garden State" in honor of New Jersey's tercentenary.

[19]"Program of Preliminary Competitions"; Transcribed from the 1964 MAP video tape.

[20]Frank Prendergast, "Minn., Calif. Capture Talent and Swimsuit," ACP, 10 Sept. 1964: 1; Observations of the 1964 MAP by the investigator.

[21]"Program of Preliminary Competitions"; Video tape observation.

[22]Video tape observation; "Program of Preliminary Competitions."

[23]"Program of Preliminary Competitions"; Videotape observations.

[24]"Preliminary Competitions."

[25]"Preliminary Competitions."

[26]*Ibid.*; Prendergast, "N. Dakotan, W. Virginian Win" 14; "Program of Preliminary Competitions"; Video tape observation; "Program of Preliminary Competitions."

[27]Video tape observation; "Program of Preliminary Competitions."

[28]Prendergast, "Minn., Calif. Capture" 1; Prendergast, "N. Dakotan, W. Virginian Win" 1; Frank J. Prendergast, "Alabama, New Mexico Win in Talent, Swimsuit," ACP, 12 Sept. 1964: 1.

[29]Frank J. Prendergast, "Miss Arizona Wins Crown," ACP, 13 Sept. 1964: 1; "Program of Finals," *1964 Miss America Pageant [Program]* 35.

[30]Frank Deford, *There She Is: The Life and Times of Miss America* (1971; New York: Viking, 1978) 207.

[31]"Program of Finals."

[32]Transcribed from the MA 1965 videotape.

[33]MA 1965 videotape.

[34]Interview with John Koushouris.

[35]Video tape observation by the investigator.

[36]Observation of 1965 MAP video tape by investigator; The order listed in "Program of Finals" differed from what actually occurred.

[37]"Miss Arizona Wins Crown"; videotape observation.

[38]Videotape observation.

[39]Observation of videotape; "Gate Crasher Interrupts Pageant Show," ACP, 13 Sept. 1964: 36.

[40]Letter from Vonda Kay Van Dyke Scoates.

[41]Vonda Kay Van Dyke Scoates.

[42]Interview with John Koushouris; Interview with John Zerbe, Miss America Pageant Executive Vice President, 27 Feb. 1987.

[43]Interview with John Koushouris.

[44]"1966," *Show Statistics; Letter from Lenora Slaughter Frapart (NYU Media Survey 2) 7 August 1987; "1967," Show Statistics*; Deford 331; *A 40 Year Report.*


*Chapter VIII*

[1]*A 40 Year Report of The Miss America Scholarship Pageant Scholarship Foundation 1945-1985*, booklet provided by the Miss America Pageant Office.

[2]Interview with Laurel Schaefer, 12 Sept. 1986.

[3]In Susan Brownmiller, *Femininity* (New York: Linden, 1984) 24-25; Judy Klemesrud, "Miss America: She's Always on the Road," NYT, 4 July 1974: 9; The author was an undergraduate student at Montclair State at this time and also a featured entertainer at the pageant.

[4]Ellen O'Brien, "NOW Parade: Women United," *The Press* (TP), 8 Sept. 1974: 1, A2.

[5]Carlo Sardella, " 'Miss America' Faces Ms.," NYT, 1 Sept. 1974: 47; Interview with Jacqueline Walker, one of the organizers of the 1974 Atlantic City NOW Convention, 6 Sept. 1988.

[6]Judy Klemesrud, "For Miss America '75, the Questions Get Tougher," NYT, 9 Sept. 1974: 40.

[7]Klemesrud, "Miss America: She's Always on the Road" 9.

[8]Klemesrud, "For Miss America '75" 40.

[9]Ellen O'Brien, "Pageant Beauties Strict on Rape, Prostitution," TP, 3 Sept. 1974: 11; "Miss America State Representatives," [*1974*] *Miss America Pageant* [program] 63; Suzanne Dolezal, "Miss America's Robes to Stay in Mothballs," TP, 3 Sept. 1974: 1, 10.

[10]"1972," *Miss America Pageant Show Statistics 1951-[1985]*, unpublished document provided by the MAP offices.

[11]"Miss America Pageant Show."

[12]Frank Deford, *There She Is: The Life and Times of Miss America* (1971; New York: Viking, 1972) 330-31.

[13]"25 Bands, 28 Floats In Parade," *The Press (TP)*, 3 Sept. 1974: 1, 12; Susan Dolezal and Gail Seider, "Walk Parade Lures 150,000 In Chilly Rain," TP, 4 Sept. 1974: 1, 14.

[14]"Boardwalk Parade," [*1974*] *Miss America Pageant* [program] 15.

[15]"25 Bands, 28 Floats In Parade"; "Walk Parade Lures 150,000 In Chilly Rain"; Gail Seider, "Iowa Band Here to Honor Alumnus," TP, 3 Sept. 1974.

[16]Dolezal and Seider, "Walk Parade"; "Pageant Float Winners," TP, 4 Sept. 1974: 1.

[17]This conclusion is based on the following data: "Program of Preliminary Competitions," [1974] Miss America Pageant [program] 33; "Program of Finals," [1974] Miss America Pageant [program] 35; Video tape observations of the 1974 MAP.

[18]Suzanne Dolezal, "Their Talent is Major Factor," TP, 7 Sept. 1974: 8.

[19]According to "Program of Preliminary Competitions" 33: "Mu Alpha Sigma is the official sorority of all National Miss America Representatives."

[20][1974] Miss America Pageant [program] 28-29.

[21]"Program of Preliminaries"; video tape observation.

[22]Video tape observation.

[23]Video tape observation; "Program of Preliminaries."

[24]Video tape observation; "Program of Preliminaries."

[25]Video tape observation.

[26]Video tape observations; "Program of Preliminaries."

[27]Video tape observations.

[28]Video tape observation; "Program of Preliminaries."

[29]Suzanne Dolezal and Gale Seider, "Tennessee and Kansas Win at Pageant," TP, 5 Sept. 1974: 1; Suzanne Dolezal and Gale Seider, "Kentucky, Texas Win 2nd Night," TP, 6 Sept. 1974: 1; Suzanne Dolezal and Gale Seider, "Ill., Calif. Win Talent, Swimsuit," TP, 7 Sept. 1974: 1, 3.

[30]Gale Seider, "Plans for Show Begin Early," TP, 5 Sept. 1974: 12; Interview with Joe Cook, 11 Sept. 1986.

[31]Gale Seider, "Plans for Show Begin Early."

[32]Seider.

[33]Seider.

[34]Telephone interview with Therese Hanley, Miss New Jersey 1980, 15 May 1988.

[35]Interview with Joe Cook.

[36]"Program of Finals," [1974] Miss America Pageant [program] 35; "1974," Miss America Pageant National Show Statistics 1951-1985, unpublished document provided by the Miss America Pageant offices.

[37]"Program of Finals," The [1974] Miss America Pageant [program] 35.

[38]Video tape observation; Interviews with Cook and Koushouris.

[39]Video tape observation of 1974 MAP.

[40]Video tape observation; "Program of Finals."

[41]Video tape observation.

[42]Video tape observation.

[43]The speech made by Albert Marks was transcribed from the 1974 MAP video tape.

[44]Interview with Joe Cook.

[45]Deford 306.

[46]There was a break for two commercials after every two contestants. Video tape observation; "Program of Finals."

[47]Video tape observation.

[48]This "last look" consisted of a slow pan from screen right to screen left.

[49]Video tape observation.

[50]Video tape observation.

### Chapter IX

[1]"1980," Miss America Pageant Show Statistics 1951-[1985], unpublished document provided by the MAP offices.

[2]Lisa DePaulo, "Mr. Miss America," *Atlantic City* September 1986: 45.

[3]"1982," *Miss America Pageant Show Statistics 1951-[1985]*, unpublished document provided by the MAP offices; "1980," *Show Statistics*.

[4]Mary Flanagan, "Embarrassing Moments for Miss America," TP, 11 Sept. 1984: 28.

[5]*Oh, God* was the title of a current George Burns movie. "Here She Comes, Miss America," Pictorial, Photos by Tom Chiapel, no author for copy, *Penthouse* September 1984: 66-75; Bob Guccione, "Tom Chiapel [Interview]," *Penthouse* November 1984: 89. The caption on the cover read "More Vanessa Williams"; "Bound For Glory," Pictorial, photos by Jonathan Michael Aaron, no author for copy, *Penthouse* January 1985: 52-61.

[6]Randy Diamond, Clint Rosewell, and Stuart Marques, "Vanessa Set to Lose Title," *The [New York] Daily News* 21 July 1984: 3; A list of MAs in the 1984 program shows William's reign as being from September 17, 1983—July 23, 1984, with Charles reigning from July 23, 1984—September 15, 1984. "Miss Americas in Review," *The 1984 Miss America Pageant* [program]: 64.

[7]Mary Flanagan, "Pageant Gets Last Laugh at Scandal," TP, 11 Sept. 1984: 1.

[8]Mary Flanagan, "Pageant Gets Last Laugh"; Lucia Calascibetta, "Media Magnify Pageant's Magnificence," TP, 11 Sept. 1984: 22; Michael Wald, "Pageant Draws Protest from Two Small Groups," TP, 16 Sept. 1984: A16.

[9]Joseph Tanfani, "Court Case Haunts Miss Ohio," TP, 12 Sept. 1984: 1.

[10]As said to this investigator by various former Miss Americas and pageant organizers during interviews.

[11]Mary Flanagan and Lucia Calascibetta, "Parade Dazzles 200,000," TP, 12 Sept. 1984: 1.

[12]Barton Jones, "Creative Caravan Contains Convertibles, Camel," TP, 11 Sept. 1984: P4.

[13]Jones, P8.

[14]Mary Flanagan and Lucia Calascibetta, "Parade Dazzles" 1.

[15]Barton Jones, "New Coordinators Make Changes in Pageant Parade," TP, 11 Sept. 1984: P21; Flanagan and Calascibetta, "Parade Dazzles" 10.

[16]Flanagan and Calascibetta, "Parade Dazzles" 11.

[17]Virginia Mann, "Beyond the Runway: Scenes of the Competition Unseen," *The Record* 9 Sept. 1988: 5.

[18]Data about the origin of this tradition was obtained by the investigator from anonymous sources in Atlantic City's gay community. The exact year this custom began is unknown.

[19]Flanagan and Calascibetta, "Parade Dazzles" 1, 11.

[20]Jones, "Creative Caravans" P4; Flanagan and Calascibetta, "Parade Dazzles" 1.

[21]A summary of the specific content will be included under the following sub-section, *The 1984 Finals*; "Program of Preliminary Competitions," *The 1984 Miss America Pageant* [program]: 31.

[22]Interview with John Koushouris.

[23]Koushouris.

[24]Koushouris.

[25]*Ibid.*; Video tape observation of the 1984 MAP by the investigator.

[26]Joseph Tanfani and Mary Flanagan, "Texas, Mass. Winners," TP, 13 Sept. 1984: 1, 10; Lucia Calascibetta and Joseph Tanfani, "New York, Utah Win Prelim," TP, 14 Sept. 1984: 1, 10; Mary Flanagan and Lucia Calascibetta, "It's Minnesota, Mississippi," TP, 15 Sept. 1984: 1, 12.

[27]"Program of Finals," *The 1984 Miss America Pageant* [program]: 35.

[28]Lucia Calascibetta, Joseph Tanfani and Mary Flanagan, "Miss Utah Takes Crown," TP, 16 Sept. 1984: 1.

[29]Transcribed from the 1984 MAP video tape.

[30]Video tape observation; "Program of Finals"; Interview with John Koushouris.

[31]In his interview, John Koushouris acknowledged that the show is staged with the home audience in mind; Video tape observation and live observation.

[32]Video tape and live observation.

[33]Video tape and live observation.

[34]Interview with Jean Bray, 12 Sept. 1986.

[35]Video tape and live observation.

[36]Video tape and live observation; "Program of Finals."

[37]"Program of Finals"; Video and live observation.

[38]Video and live observation; Peggy Moran, "Here She Comes, Broke," *Atlantic City [Magazine]* September 1987: 47; "Program of Finals."

[39]Video tape and live observation; "Program of Finals."

[40]Interview with John Koushouris.

[41]Joseph Tanfani, "Pageant Show Gets Injection of Satire," TP, 12 Sept. 1984: 12; Video and live observations; "Program of Finals."

[42]Video and live observations; "Program of Finals."

[43]Video and live observation.

[44]Video and live observation.

[45]Video and live observation.

[46]Calascibetta, Tanfani, Flanagan, "Miss Utah" 1.

[47]"Miss America May Lose Crown," *New York Post* 4 Sept. 1985: 3.

[48]Video and live observations.

[49]David Zimmerman, "A Squeaky-Clean Miss America," *USA Today* 17 Sept. 1984: 1D; Don Singleton, "Sharlene Wells is Model of Decorum," NYDN, 17 Sept. 1984: 3.

[50]Letter from Sharlene Wells Hawkes, 10 August 1988.

[51]Interview with Laura Bridges and Therese Hanley, October 1989; Interview with Patricia LaTerra, Miss New Jersey 1984, on *Panorama*, Prime Cable of New Jersey, August 1985.

[52]As recorded from the 1990 telecast.

### Chapter X

[1]Further, in-depth analysis of the impact of television on the *Miss America Pageant* can be found in Riverol, A., *The Miss America Pageant: A Comparative Structural Analysis of the Pre- and Post-Television Event* New York University, 1988, the doctoral dissertation upon which much of this book is based. This dissertation is also on file at Miss America Headquarters in Atlantic City.

[2]"125 Stations to Carry Live Pageant Telecast," 7 Sept. 1954: 1.

[3]"Miss America: Scandals Don't Boost Viewership," *The New York Post* 18 Sept. 1984: 93.

[4]Interview with John Koushouris, MAP producer, 15 May 1987.

[5]Frank Deford, *There She Is: The Life and Times of Miss America* (1971; New York: Viking, 1978) 310-311.

[6]Deford.

[7]"Miss America May Lose Saturday Night Date," *New York Post* 4 Sept. 1985: 3.

[8]Interview with Albert Marks, 12 Sept. 1986; Interview with John Koushouris.

[9]"Miss America Started in 1921 as Fall Frolic—But now is a Great Boon to Education," in the *1950 Miss America Pageant Yearbook*; Gale Seider, "Plans for Show Begin Early," *The Press* 5 Sept. 1974: 12; "1984," *Miss America Pageant National Show Statistics 1951-[1985]*, unpublished document provided by the MAP offices.

[10]Edmund Carpenter, "The New Languages," *Explorations in Communications* (Boston: Beacon Press, 1960) 176.

[11]See Harold A. Innis, *The Bias of Communication* (Toronto: U of Toronto P, 1951) 33.

[12]Innis 33.

[13]Based on Marshall McLuhan, *The Medium is the Message* (New York: Bantam, 1967) 63.

[14]Video tape observations and timing of the 1964, 1974, 1984 and 1988 MAPs; Interview with John Koushouris.

[15]See Michael Real, *Mass Mediated Culture* (New York: Prentice, 1977) for a discussion on dramatic structure of events.

[16]Interview with Karen Aarons, Executive Director of MAP Field Operations, 27 Feb. 1987.

[17]Deford 309.

# Works Cited

*Books, Magazines, Newspapers and Other Studies*

Aaron, Jonathan Michael. "Bound For Glory." Pictorial. *Penthouse* January 1985: 52-61.

Advertisement. *Atlantic City Press.* 8 September 1964.

Advertisement (for tickets). *The Press* 11 September 1984: P8.

*A 40 Year Report of The Miss America Scholarship Pageant Scholarship Foundation 1945-1985.* Booklet provided by the Miss America Pageant Office.

" 'American Beauty Special' to Bring 33 Pageant Girls." *Atlantic City Press* 7 September 1943: 1.

"Atlantic City to Drop Its Outdoor Pageant." *New York Times* 12 March 12 1928: 13.

Atlantic Foto Service, untitled photograph. *Atlantic City Daily Press* 8 September 1921: 1.

"Attack Beauty Pageant." *New York Times* 1 March 1927: 3.

"Attacks Bathing Review." *New York Times* 11 September 1923: 15.

Barry, Constance. "NOW Gets Going." *The Press* 7 September 1974: 1.

Banner, Lois. *American Beauty.* New York: Knopf, 1983.

"Bathers' Revue." *Atlantic City Daily Press* 9 September 1921: 1.

Beach, Edward P. "Epidemic of Beauty About to Hit Town." *Atlantic City Daily Press* 4 September 1922: 1.

———. "Resort Fairly Bulges Beauty for Big Fete." *Atlantic City Daily Press* 5 September 1923: 1.

"Beauties Arrive at Shore Pageant." *New York Times* 2 September 1924.

"Beauty Queen Chosen." *New York Times* 5 October 1934: 7.

"Beauty Title Lines Field Against N.Y." *Atlantic City Daily Press* 9 September 1933: 12.

"Bewildering Display of Beauty Gives Great Multitude a Thrill Along 'Walk." *Atlantic City Daily Press* 7 September 1923: 1.

"Bishop Condemns Beauty Pageant." *New York Times* 30 November 1927: 10.

"Boardwalk Spectacle Will Be Staged Tomorrow if Weather Permits." *Atlantic City Press* 6 September 1935: 1.

Boorstin, Daniel J. *The Image.* New York: Antheum, 1980.

Boucher, John L. "Miss Florida First Runner-Up." *Atlantic City Press* 12 September 1954: 1, 18.

———. "Miss Florida Wins Swim Suit Event." *Atlantic City Press* 10 September 1954.

———. "6,000 Attend First Night of Preliminary Judging." *Atlantic City Press* 9 September 1954: 1.

———. "6,100 View Final Preliminary." *Atlantic City Press* 11 September 1954: 1.

"Bronx Girl Chosen in Bathing-Suit Event in Atlantic City." *New York Times* 5 September 1935: 25.

Brownmiller, Susan. *Femininity.* New York: Linden, 1984.

Calascibetta, Lucia. "Media Magnify Pageant's Magnificence." *The Press* 11 September 1984: 22.

—— and Joseph Tanfani. "New York, Utah Win Prelim." *The Press* 14 September 1984: 1, 10.

—— and Mary Flanagan. "Miss Utah Takes Crown." *The Press* 16 September 1984: 1.

Caldwell, Kate. "There She Grows...Miss America Packs on Hefty 20 Lbs." *Star* 12 February 1991: 6.

Capetini, Roger. "Miss America Stole My Husband." *National Enquirer* 12 February 1991: 51.

Carpenter, Edmund. "The New Languages." *Explorations in Communications.* Boston: Beacon P, 1960.

Chiapel, Tom. "Here She Comes, Miss America." Pictorial. *Penthouse* September 1984: 66-75.

"Complete Prize List." *Atlantic City Daily Press* 9 September 1921: 1.

Crawford, Ollie. "Blonde Jean Bartel New Beauty Queen." *Atlantic City Press* 12 September 1943: 1.

—— "Miss California is Again Winner." *Atlantic City Press* 11 September 1943: 1.

"Criticism Well Deserved." *New York Times* April 1924: 16.

"Crowd Goes Wild Over Marvelous Spectacle Two Miles in Length." *Atlantic City Daily Press* 8 September 1922: 1.

"Curtain Rolls Back on Big Pageant—Beauties Captivate Great Throngs." *Atlantic City Daily Press* 7 September 1921: 7.

Deford, Frank. *There She Is: The Life and Times of Miss America.* New York: Viking, 1978.

DePaulo, Lisa. "Mr. Miss America." *Atlantic City* September 1986: 45.

Diamond, Randy, Clint Rosewell, and Stuart Marques. "Vanessa Set to Lose Title." *New York Daily News* 21 July 1984: 3.

Dolezal, Suzanne. "Miss America's Robes to Stay in Mothballs." *The Press* 3 September 1974: 1, 10.

—— "Their Talent is Major Factor." *The Press* 7 September 1974: 8.

—— and Gale Seider. "Ill., Calif. Win Talent, Swimsuit." *The Press* 7 September 1974: 1, 3.

—— "Kentucky, Texas Win 2nd Night." *The Press* 6 September 1974: 1.

—— "Tennessee and Kansas Win at Pageant." *The Press* 5 September 1974: 1.

—— "Walk Parade Lures 150,000 In Chilly Rain." *The Press* 4 September 1974: 1, 14.

Dworkin, Susan. *Miss America 1945: Bess Myerson's Own Story.* New York: New Market Press, 1987.

"Fall Carnival Holds Sway in Atlantic City." *New York Times* 6 September 1923: 28.

Flanagan, Mary. "Embarrassing Moments for Miss America." *The Press* 11 September 1984: 28.

—— "Pageant Gets Last Laugh at Scandal." *The Press* 11 September 1984: 1.

—— and Lucia Calascibetta. "It's Minnesota, Mississippi." *The Press* 15 September 1984: 1, 12.

—— "Parade Dazzles 200,000." *The Press* 12 September 1984: 1.

Funnel, Charles E. *By the Beautiful Sea: The Rise and High Times of that Great Resort, Atlantic City.* Rutgers, NJ: Rutgers U P, 1983.

"Gate Crasher Interrupts Pageant Show." *Atlantic City Press* 13 September 1964: 36.

Giedion, Siegfried. *Mechanization Takes Command*. New York: Norton, 1975.

Gill, Brendan. "The Miss America Uproar: What it Says About us All." *TV Guide* September 15-21, 1984.

"Girl Makes Dash From Alaska to Enter Pageant Tournament." *Atlantic City Daily Press* 2 September 1922: 1.

Goldman, William. *Hype and Glory*. New York: Villard, 1991.

Goodman, Ellen. "Miss America Paid the Price For Crossing the Line Between Pageantry and Pornography." *The Hudson [New Jersey] Dispatch* 31 July 1984: 11.

"Gorgeous Beauty Feature of Climaxing Spectacles in City's Great Pageant." *Atlantic City Daily Press* 9 September 1921: 1.

Gorn, Janice. *The Writer's Handbook*. New York: Monarch, 1984.

"Grand Prize Award in Division No. 6." *Atlantic City Daily Press* 5 September 1921: 1.

Guccione, Bob. "Tom Chiapel: Interview." *Penthouse* November 1984: 89.

"Here's How Pageant Picks Miss America." *Atlantic City Press* 10 September 1964: 7.

"Hudson Maxim to be Father Neptune." *Atlantic City Daily Press* 5 September 1921.

Innis, Harold A. *The Bias of Communication*. Toronto: U of Toronto P, 1951.

Jagmetty, Victor. "Beach Combers." *Atlantic City Daily Press* 7 September 1921: 9.

Jones, Barton. "Creative Caravan Contains Convertibles, Camel." *The Press* 11 September 1984: P4.

———. "New Coordinators Make Changes in Pageant Parade." *The Press* 11 September 1984: P21.

"King Neptune Opens Seashore Pageant." *New York Times* 7 September 1922: 26.

Klemesrud, Judy. "Can Feminists Upstage Miss America?" *New York Times* 8 September 1974: 58.

———. "For Miss America '75, the Questions Get Tougher." *New York Times* 9 September 1974: 40.

———. "Miss America: She's Always on the Road." *New York Times* 4 July 1974: 9.

Levi, Vicki Gold, and Lee Eisenberg. *Atlantic City: 125 Years of Ocean Madness*. New York: Clarkson N. Potter, 1979.

"Lineup for Today's Pageant Parade." *Atlantic City Press* 8 September 1953: 11.

Mann, Virginia. "Beyond the Runway: Scenes of the Competition Unseen." *The Record* 9 September 1988: 5.

Martin, Nancie. *Miss America Through the Looking Glass: The Story Behind the Scenes*. New York: Simon and Schuster, 1985.

Marques, Stuart. "Whooosh!—Miss America Ducks Press on Her Return." *New York Daily News* 21 July 1984: 3.

"May Reported Ill: Owen Pageant Emcee." *Atlantic City Press* 11 September 1953: 1.

McLaughlin, Peter, and Stuart Marques. "Vanessa Set to Fess Up." *New York Daily News* 22 July 1984: 5.

McLuhan, Marshall. *The Medium is the Message*. New York: Bantam, 1967.

McMahon, William. *So Young...So Gay*. Atlantic City: Atlantic City P, 1970.

Mercer, Jacques. *How to Win a Beauty Contest*. Phoenix: Curran, 1960.

Milloy, Ross. "Almost Miss America." *TV Guide* September 4-10, 1982.

"Miss America Beauty, Health, and Talent Pageant." *New York Times* 5 September 1943: 10.

"Miss America Exposed: Vanessa the Undressa." *New York Daily News* 21 July 1984: 21.

"Miss America May Lose Crown." *New York Post* 4 September 1985: 3.

"Miss America of 1954 to Go Shopping Here." *New York Times* 14 September 1953: 17.

"Miss America Pageant Started in 1921 as a Fall Frolic—But Now is a Great Boon to Education." *Miss America Pageant Yearbook* 1950.

"Miss America Standards Have Changed Throughout the Years." *Atlantic City Press* 7 September 1954: 6.

"Miss Atlantic City Greeter 'Humiliated,' Quits Post." *Atlantic City Press* 10 September 1964: 21.

"Miss Boston Triumphs Again." *Atlantic City Press* 10 September 1943: 22.

"Miss California First To Score." *Atlantic City Press* 9 September 1943: 10.

"Miss California Wins." *New York Times* 4 September 1935: 22.

"Miss Congeniality." *Atlantic City Press* 12 September 1954: 18.

"Miss Indianapolis is Prettiest Girl." *New York Times* 8 September 1922: 20.

"Miss Manhattan Scores." *New York Times* 5 September 1924: 6.

"Miss New York Wins Gold Cup for Pageant Girls." *Atlantic City Daily Press* 8 September 1933: 1.

"Miss Pittsburgh Wins Beauty Crown." *New York Times* 8 September 1935: 25.

"Miss Washington Carries Away Golden Mermaid." *Atlantic City Daily Press* 9 September 1921: 12.

Moran, Peggy. "Here She Comes, Broke." *Atlantic City Magazine* September 1987: 49.

Morgan, Robin. "The Vanessa Williams Controversy: What's a Feminist to Think?" *Ms.* October 1984: 154.

Moses, Peter, and Larry Nathanson. "Favorite Daughter Still Reigns in Home Town." *New York Post* 21 July 1984: 3.

"Neptune Arrives, Waves Magic Trident, and Super Carnival Grips Resort." *Atlantic City Daily Press* 8 September 8 1921.

Nichols, Harmon W. "Beauty Sets School Talk." *Atlantic City Press* 10 September 1953: 1, 12.

———— "Boardwalk No-Man's Land As Pageant Girls Arrive." *Atlantic City Press* 8 September 1953: 11.

"Night Carnival Draws Great Crowd to 'Walk." *Atlantic City Daily Press* 8 September 1921: 1.

"1956." *Miss America Pageant Show Statistics 1951-[1985].* Unpublished document provided by the Miss America Pageant offices.

"1957." *Miss America Pageant Show Statistics 1951-[1985].* Unpublished document provided by the Miss America Pageant offices.

"1960." *Miss America Pageant Show Statistics 1951-[1985].* Unpublished document provided by the Miss America Pageant offices.

"1961." *Miss America Pageant Show Statistics 1951-[1985].* Unpublished document provided by the Miss America Pageant offices.

"1962." *Miss America Pageant Show Statistics 1951-[1985].* Unpublished document provided by the Miss America Pageant offices.

"1963." *Miss America Pageant Show Statistics 1951-[1985].* Unpublished document provided by the Miss America Pageant offices.

"1966." *Miss America Pageant Show Statistics 1951-[1985]*. Unpublished document provided by the Miss America Pageant offices.

"1967." *Miss America Pageant Show Statistics 1951-[1985]*. Unpublished document provided by the Miss America Pageant offices.

"1970." *Miss America Pageant Show Statistics 1951-[1985]*. Unpublished document provided by the Miss America Pageant offices.

"1971." *Miss America Pageant Show Statistics 1951-[1985]*. Unpublished document provided by the Miss America Pageant offices.

"1972." *Miss America Pageant Show Statistics 1951-[1985]*. Unpublished document provided by the Miss America Pageant offices.

"1973." *Miss America Pageant Show Statistics 1951-[1985]*. Unpublished document provided by the Miss America Pageant offices.

"1974." *Miss America Pageant National Show Statistics 1951-1985*. Unpublished document provided by the Miss America Pageant offices.

"1975." *Miss America Pageant Show Statistics 1951-[1985]*. Unpublished document provided by the Miss America Pageant offices.

"1978." *Miss America Pageant Show Statistics 1951-[1985]*. Unpublished document provided by the Miss America Pageant offices.

"1980." *Miss America Pageant Show Statistics 1951-[1985]*. Unpublished document provided by the Miss America Pageant offices.

"1981." *Miss America Pageant Show Statistics 1951-[1985]*. Unpublished document provided by the Miss America Pageant offices.

"1982." *Miss America Pageant Show Statistics 1951-[1985]*. Unpublished document provided by the Miss America Pageant offices.

"NOW'll Be Wet During Crowning." *The Press* 4 September 1974: 14.

O'Brien, Ellen. "NOW Parade: Women United." *The Press* 8 September 1974: 1, A2.

———. "Pageant Beauties Strict on Rape, Prostitution." *The Press* 3 September 1974: 11.

"125 Stations to Carry Live Pageant Telecast." *Atlantic City Press* 7 September 1954: 1.

"Organizations May Enter If Costume Worn." *Atlantic City Daily Press* 5 September 1921: 1.

"Pageant at Atlantic City." *New York Times* 1 September 1924: 24.

"Pageant Beauties Arrive in Phila[delphia] Today, Due Here Tuesday Noon." *Atlantic City Press* 6 September 1943: 1, 8.

"Pageant Beauty Ball Colorful Fete; Natty Morris Guards Act as Escorts." *Atlantic City Daily Press* 7 September 1933: 12.

"Pageant Film Popular." *Atlantic City Daily Press* 10 September 1921: 1.

"Pageant Float Winners." *The Press* 4 September 1974: 1.

"Pageant Ice Skater Without Ice Piles Up Trouble for Backers." *Atlantic City Press* 11 September 1943: 10.

"Pageant in Wide Favor With Many Urging Longer Duration of the Frolic." *Atlantic City Daily Press* 10 September 1921: 1.

"Pageant Parade Winners." *Atlantic City Press* 9 September 1953: 1.

"Pageant Program." *Atlantic City Daily Press* 7 September 1921: 1.

"Pageant Sidelights." *Atlantic City Press* 10 September 1953: 1, 12.

Panati, Charles. *Extraordinary Origins of Everyday Things*. New York: Harper and Row, 1987.

Pang, Henry. "Miss America: An American Ideal." *Journal of Popular Culture* Spring 1969: 695.

"Parade Winners." *Atlantic City Press* 9 September 1964: 1.

Postman, Neil. *Teaching as a Conserving Activity.* New York: Dell, 1979.

Prendergast, Frank J. "Alabama, New Mexico Win in Talent, Swimsuit." *Atlantic City Press* 12 September 1964: 1.

———— "Minn., Calif. Capture Talent and Swimsuit." *Atlantic City Press* 10 September 1964: 1.

———— "Miss Arizona Wins Crown." *Atlantic City Press* 13 September 1964: 1.

———— "N. Dakotan, W. Virginian Win in Talent, Swim Suit." *Atlantic City Press* 11 September 1964: 14.

———— "150,000 See Colorful Pageant Parade." *Atlantic City Press* 9 September 1964: 1.

"Press Scoops." *Atlantic City Daily Press* 9 September 1921: 1.

Prewitt, Cheryl with Kathryn Stalby. *A Bright Shining Place: The Story of a Miracle.* New York: Doubleday, 1981.

Real, Michael. *Mass Mediated Culture.* New York: Prentice, 1977.

"Resort Fairly Bulges Beauty for Big Fete." *Atlantic City Daily Press* 5 September 1923: 1.

Sardella, Carlo. "Boardwalk Jammed." *Atlantic City Press* 9 September 1953: 1.

———— "Delaware Wins in Talent." 12 September 1953: 1.

———— "Eddie Fisher Heads March Throngs Hail Arriving Girls." *Atlantic City Press* 8 September 1953: 1.

———— "5,800 Watch As Pennsylvania Wins in Swimming Suit and Virginia in Talent Competition." *Atlantic City Press* 12 September 1953: 1, 12.

———— " 'Miss America' Faces Ms." *New York Times* 1 September 1974: 47, 54.

———— "Miss Pennsylvania New Miss America." *Atlantic City Press* 13 September 1953: 7.

———— "Pageant Thrills Film Star Judge." *Atlantic City Press* 11 September 1953: 1.

———— "Resort Ripples." *Atlantic City Press* 14 September 1953: 11.

———— "S. Dakota, Wyoming Win Honors." 11 September 1953: 1.

Schor, Sam. "Famous Miss America Pageant, Miss Slaughter Masterminds." *Atlantic City Press* 8 September 1953: 11.

———— "Pageant Parade Sidelights." *Atlantic City Press* 8 September 1954: 1.

"Scores of Beauties Headed for Pageant." *New York Times* 5 September 1922.

Seider, Gale. "Iowa Band Here to Honor Alumnus." *The Press* 3 September 1974.

———— "Plans for Show Begin Early." *The Press* 5 September 1974: 12.

Singleton, Don. "Sharlene Wells is Model of Decorum." *New York Daily News* 17 September 1984: 3.

"Some Behind-Time Knocking." *Atlantic City Daily Press* 1 September 1925: 13.

"Stage, Screen Offers Made Miss America." *Atlantic City Daily Press* 11 September 1933.

Tanfani, Joseph. "Court Case Haunts Miss Ohio." *The Press* 12 September 1984: 1.

———— "Pageant Show Gets Injection of Satire." *The Press* 12 September 1984: 12.

———— and Mary Flanagan. "Texas, Mass. Winners." *The Press* 13 September 1984: 1, 10.

Test, Herb. "Bathers' Revue Unique Among Pageant Fetes." *Atlantic City Daily Press* 7 September 1921: 1.

"The Chair Parade." *Atlantic City Daily Press* 9 September 1921: 1.

"There She Goes—Miss America is Told to Quit." *New York Daily News* 21 July 1984: 1.

"30 Beauties Open Pageant for '33 Title." *Atlantic City Daily Press* 6 September 1933: 1.

"Three-Ply Holiday Gives Resort Mighty Guest List." *Atlantic City Daily Press* 4 September 1922: 1.

"Today's Jubilee Program." *Atlantic City Press* 6 September 1935: 1.

"Today's Pageant Events." *Atlantic City Daily Press* 9 September 1933: 1.

"Today's Pageant Program." *Atlantic City Daily Press* 8 September 1922: 1.

"Today's Pageant Program." *Atlantic City Daily Press* 7 September 1933: 1.

"Today's Pageant Program." *Atlantic City Press* 11 September 1953: 3.

"Today's Program." *Atlantic City Daily Press* 6 September 1933: 1.

Tomlinson, Jim. "Innovations to Put Zip Into Pageant." *Atlantic City Press* 5 September 1954: 1.

"25 Bands, 28 Floats in Parade." *The Press* 3 September 1974: 1, 12.

"Vanessa the Undressa Loses Crown." *New York Post* 21 July 1984: 1.

Villers, Ralph. "200,000 Persons Watch Beauties." *Atlantic City Press* 8 September 1954: 28.

Wald, Michael. "Pageant Draws Protest from Two Small Groups." *The Press* 16 September 1984: A16.

"Walk Parade Will Start at 8:30 P.M." *Atlantic City Press* 7 September 1954: 1.

"Why Not Enter the Bathers' Revue?" *Atlantic City Daily Press* 5 September 1921: 9.

"Women Open Fight on Beauty Pageant." *New York Times* 18 November 1927: 12.

"Won By A Nose." *New York Daily News* 15 September 1982: 2.

Zimmerman, David. "A Squeaky-Clean Miss America." *USA Today* 17 September 1984: 1D.


*Programs*

"Boardwalk Parade." *[1974] Miss America Pageant*: 15.

"Foreword." *1953 Souvenir Book of the Miss America Pageant*: 1.

"Miss Americas in Review." *The [1984] Miss America Pageant*: 64.

"Miss America State Representatives." *[1974] Miss America Pageant*: 63.

"1953 Miss America Pageant Program of Events." *[1953] Miss America Souvenir Book*: 24-25.

"Program of Final Contest." *[1954] Miss America Pageant*: 27.

"Program of Finals." *[1964] Miss America Pageant*: 35.

"Program of Finals." *[1974] Miss America Pageant*: 35.

"Program of Finals." *The [1984] Miss America Pageant*: 35.

"Program of Preliminary Competitions." *[1964] Miss America Pageant*: 31.

"Program of Preliminary Competitions." *[1974] Miss America Pageant*: 33.

"Program of Preliminary Competitions." *The [1984] Miss America Pageant*: 31.

"Program of Preliminary Contests." *[1954] Miss America Pageant*: 24-25.

St. John, Louis. "In the Twenties." *1960 Miss America Pageant Yearbook*: np.

_____ "In 1935." *The 1960 Miss America Pageant Yearbook*: 9.

_____ "In 1936." *The 1960 Miss America Pageant Yearbook*: 11.

_____ "1937 History." *The 1960 Miss America Pageant Yearbook*: 13.

_____ "In 1938." *The 1960 Miss America Pageant Yearbook*: 15.

_____ "In 1939." *The 1960 Miss America Pageant Yearbook*: 17.

_____ "In 1941." *1960 Miss America Pageant Yearbook*: 21.

_____ "In 1943." *1960 Miss America Pageant Yearbook*: 25.

_____ "In 1947." *1960 Miss America Pageant Yearbook*: 33.

_____ "In 1948." *1960 Miss America Pageant Yearbook*: 34.

_____ "In 1949." *1960 Miss America Pageant Yearbook*: 35.

_____ "In 1950." *1960 Miss America Pageant Yearbook*: 39.

_____ "In 1953." *1960 Miss America Pageant Yearbook*: 45.

_____ "In 1954." *1960 Miss America Pageant Yearbook*: 47.

_____ "In 1955." *The 1960 Miss America Pageant Yearbook*: 49.

_____ "In 1957." *The 1957 Miss America Pageant Yearbook*: 52.

_____ "In 1958." *The 1960 Miss America Pageant Yearbook*: 57.

_____ "In 1959." *The 1960 Miss America Pageant Yearbook*: 59.

"The Silver Anniversary of the Miss Americas." *1951 Miss America Pageant Yearbook*: np.

*Correspondence and Interviews*

Aarons, Karen. Executive Secretary and Director of Field Operations for the Miss America Pageant. February 27, 1987.

Bridges, Laura. October 1989.

Bray, Jean. Miss America Pageant Press Chairperson. September 12, 1986.

Cook, Joe. Miss America Pageant writer. September 11, 1986.

Frapart, Lenora S. Slaughter. August 7, 1987.

Hanley, Therese. Miss New Jersey 1980. Telephone interview, May 15, 1988; Personal interview, October 1989.

Hawkes, Sharlene Wells. August 10, 1984.

Koushouris, John. Miss America Pageant Producer. May 15, 1987.

LaTerra, Patricia. Interview on *Panorama*. Prime Cable of New Jersey. August 1985.

McKnight, Marian Bergeron. August 11, 1987.

Meriwether, Lee. August 11, 1987.

Phillips, Adrian. August 7, 1987.

Schaefer, Laurel. Miss America 1972. September 12, 1986.

Scoates, Vonda Kay Van Dyke. August 31, 1987.

Seber, Jean. Miss America Pageant Press Chairperson. September 12, 1986.

Sempier, Evelyn Ay. Miss America 1954. September 13, 1986.

Walker, Jacqueline. Organizer of the 1974 Atlantic City National Organization of Women (NOW) Convention. September 6, 1988.

Zerbe, John. Miss America Pageant Executive Vice President. February 27, 1987.

*Video Tapes*

The 1958 *Miss America Pageant*.

The 1964 *Miss America Pageant*.

The 1974 *Miss America Pageant*.

The 1982 *Miss America Pageant*.

The 1983 *Miss America Pageant*.

The 1984 *Miss America Pageant*.

The 1985 *Miss America Pageant*.

The 1986 *Miss America Pageant*.

The 1987 *Miss America Pageant*.

The 1988 *Miss America Pageant*.

The 1989 *Miss America Pageant.*
The 1990 *Miss America Pageant.*

*Documentaries*
Miss...or Myth? Geoffrey Dunn and Mark Schwartz, Directors. Dunn, Schwartz and
    Claire Rubach, Producers. Distributed by Cinema Guild, 1987.
Transcript. "The Youngest Beauty Queens." *20/20* ABC News. July 25, 1985.

# Index